52 Fights

52 *Fights*

A NEWLYWED'S CONFESSION

Jennifer Jeanne Patterson

BERKLEY BOOKS, NEW YORK

THE BERKLEY PUBLISHING GROUP
Published by the Penguin Group
Penguin Group (USA) Inc.
375 Hudson Street, New York, New York 10014, USA
Penguin Group (Canada), 10 Alcorn Avenue, Toronto, Ontario M4V 3B2, Canada
(a division of Pearson Penguin Canada Inc.)
Penguin Books Ltd., 80 Strand, London WC2R 0RL, England
Penguin Group Ireland, 25 St. Stephen's Green, Dublin 2, Ireland
(a division of Penguin Books Ltd.)
Penguin Group (Australia), 250 Camberwell Road, Camberwell, Victoria 3124, Australia
(a division of Pearson Australia Group Pty. Ltd.)
Penguin Books India Pvt. Ltd., 11 Community Centre, Panchsheel Park, New Delhi—110 017,
India
Penguin Group (NZ), Cnr. Airborne and Rosedale Roads, Albany, Auckland 1310, New Zealand
(a division of Pearson New Zealand Ltd.)
Penguin Books (South Africa) (Pty.) Ltd., 24 Sturdee Avenue, Rosebank, Johannesburg 2196,
South Africa

Penguin Books Ltd., Registered Offices: 80 Strand, London WC2R 0RL, England

This book is an original publication of The Berkley Publishing Group.

Copyright © 2005 by Jennifer Patterson Samuel.
Cover design by Tamaya Perry.

PRINTING HISTORY
Berkley trade paperback edition / June 2005

Library of Congress Cataloging-in-Publication Data

Patterson, Jennifer Jeanne.
    52 fights : a newlywed's confession / by Jennifer Jeanne Patterson.—Berkley trade pbk. ed.
      p. cm.
    Includes bibliographical references.
    ISBN 0-425-20254-2
    1. Marriage. 2. Marital conflict. 3. Married people—Psychology. 4. Patterson, Jennifer
Jeanne—Marriage. 5. Wives—Biography. I. Title: Fifty-two fights. II. Title.

    HQ734.P27 2005
    306.872—dc22   2004066024

PRINTED IN THE UNITED STATES OF AMERICA

10   9   8   7   6   5   4   3

Acknowledgments

I would like to extend special thanks to my husband, Mathias W. Samuel. Your support and encouragement mean more than you'll ever know. Many thanks to my editor, Leona Nevler, and my agent, Brettne Bloom of Kneerim & Williams, for their vision and hard work. Also, thanks to Linda Zespy and Ingrid Kane-Johnson for their insight. A debt of gratitude to all of those who generously opened up their lives to me: Anne and Pete, Brenda and Mike Applegate, Michael Florey, Brian Long, Clarence and Marguerite Samuel, Barb Skarboe, Christina and Rob Spence, and Malisa Wood. My deepest appreciation to my mother, Louise Krizek Patterson, who taught me the art of dreaming before I learned how to write. And to my father, John Lawrence Patterson, may you get stared at in your favorite diner while eating soup.

Contents

For Matt

Love is patient, love is kind.
Love envies no one, is never boastful, never conceited, never rude;
Love is never selfish, never quick to take offense
Love keeps no score of wrongs, takes no pleasure in the
sins of others, but delights in the truth.
There is nothing love cannot face; there is no limit to its faith,
its hope, its endurance.

—The Bible, 1 Corinthians 13:4–7

52 Fights: A Newlywed's Confession

By Jennifer Jeanne Patterson

I used to be the sort of woman for whom marriage seemed more like an ending—no more first dates, spontaneous driving trips alone, or taking pride in my self-sufficiency—rather than the beginning of a new way of life. There was no way I was ready to put all of my eggs in one basket for someone else to carry; I had emerged from my chaotic early twenties secure with the knowledge that I could take care of myself, and I was apprehensive about adding another person permanently to the mix. Unlike some of the more conventional heroines in popular women's novels, I did not spend my days fantasizing about engagement rings and china pattern selections. To me, marriage ultimately meant surrender, boredom, the possibility of waking up and realizing you had become the kind of woman you swore you'd never be.

But, of course, the moment I proclaimed my romantic independence, I met a wonderful man who was so different from anyone I'd dated in the past, and before I could say "planning a wedding is not my kind of thing," I was envisioning our names together on a gaudy mailbox, feeling jealous when I caught him looking at other women in the street, and nodding yes to his proposal to become his wife. Before long, I had the perfect dress, photographer, and reception location; eleven months later, on June 1, 2002, shortly after my twenty-ninth birthday, Mathias W. Samuel and I said, "I do."

Although I was elated about the idea of spending the rest of my life with Matt, a gregarious farm boy turned lawyer from North Dakota who was as comfortable at a barn kegger as he was at a wine and cheese party, the fears I had about becoming a WIFE continued to plague me from the moment he proposed. Like so many women who came of age when I did, I realized I would need to find a way to reconcile the feminist legacy I'd inherited from my mom, who had warned me against marrying young and for the wrong reasons, with that secret craving every woman I know has for the happily-ever-after fairy tale. But was such reconciliation even possible? And would I have to sacrifice my identity, my independence, or the well-being of my relationship with my husband to achieve it?

Then the plot thickened. We both lived—separately—in Minneapolis. Exactly three months before our wedding day, Matt managed to convince me that we should buy a sixties-style house in a fancy suburb outside the city. It desperately needed updating. As if dealing with the transition from single woman to wife—and from living alone to cohabitation—was not enough to give a girl hives, I was now about to plunge into a yearlong remodeling project.

* * *

This book, *52 Fights: A Newlywed's Confession*, tells the story of how Matt and I survived our first year of marriage without strangling each other. I've written about the challenges we dealt with from coping with our various incompatibilities and our very different families to the sudden absence of the romance we knew in our courtship, our encroachment on each other's personal space, and my identity crisis.

Not only is this book the story of how I learned to overcome the fears I had about my new identity, it also explores how Matt and I learned to work through our problems together. Like so many young couples I know, Matt and I spent much of our first year of marriage coming to grips with our different expectations and fears about what married life would be like for us. While Matt struggled to realize that I was not flawless and that no marriage, not even the ones he idealizes, is perfect, I stumbled over what it meant to be a "good wife." At times, we doubted that we were getting "it" right—would we become another starter marriage, a statistic?

Just when I started to wonder if Matt and I had made a big mistake, we began to find that our love and commitment to each other were building with each hurdle we surmounted. And instead of dwelling on one another's weaknesses and imperfections, we started drawing on each other's strengths. Once we realized that it was our differences that made us stronger, we stopped letting them pull us apart. And as our relationship strengthened, my fears about what it meant to trust another person with my future began to fade.

One of the key realizations that Matt and I came to after our first year of marriage: building a loving, lifelong partnership is a lot like remodeling a house. Both are works in progress, both can be messy and frustrating, and sometimes you have to tear down old walls and start from scratch in order to create something that is uniquely and wonderfully your own.

Prelude: Engaged! A Freefall

Here's to matrimony, the high sea for which
no compass has yet been invented.
—Heinrich Heine

I am standing in the entryway of the split-level suburban house
that my fiancé, Matt, and I are about to tour when I realize
that I have just encountered my worst nightmare: the homeowner
answered her front door wearing a pink and purple jogging suit,
a small white poodle tucked under her arm. I can't buy this
house. If we move to the suburbs, I could end up like her.

"No," I say to my fiancé, Matt, as soon as we're back in the
car. "No way." Her house was insufferably cheerful. And I fear
that living here in the suburbs would turn me into a willfully
subservient housewife who frets over whether the temperature
dictates linen or flannel sheets on the guest room bed.

He looks crestfallen. "But didn't you like the bar built into the
basement?" I shrug. It's true, the bar was appealing, especially because it made the house feel quirkier. But it was not enough to
compensate for my fears.

A few days later, his mom tries. Over lunch, she looks at me with her crisp, brown eyes, which I see clearly through her glasses. "You'll appreciate the garage in the winter when you have kids and you need to bring the groceries in."

Hearing this only makes things worse. Soon, they'll tell me to trade in my compact car for a Suburban. I can't breathe. It's stressful enough that I'm about to become a wife; I can't think about becoming a mother, too. At twenty-eight, I don't feel ready for the kind of genteel life that Matt, who is a lawyer and four years older than I am, envisions for us. "I need diversity," I say finally, but that is only a part of the truth. I tell Matt I want to live by the chain of lakes in Minneapolis after we're married, near most of the other young couples we know.

"What sort of diversity do you see there?" he asks. He's right; it's one of the nicer areas in the city, near half million–dollar homes. "If you want diversity, pick a different neighborhood."

Good point. I rethink mine.

I don't belong in suburbia. Growing up, I lived in upstate New York, in a duplex in downtown Ithaca, half of which my parents rented out to a single mother and her son. "I have lived the American dream," my dad told me once, because he sent all four of his daughters to college. For forty years, he worked as a lineman and drove around town in an orange bucket truck, repairing electrical wires taken down by rain storms and blizzards, just as his father had.

When I left Ithaca for Manhattan to study at Columbia University, my dad drove me there in his white Plymouth Reliant. "That's my Ivy League daughter," he said to the gas attendant, jerking his thumb at me, as we refueled. But I felt like a fraud. I never told my dad or my mom how isolated I often felt at Columbia. In the classroom, I choked on words I incorrectly pronounced. When I went home to visit my parents, I tried to show off my fancy new vocabulary, words like *poignant, verisimilitude,* and *inchoate,* which I had learned and practiced over and over again in my head during class to get the pronunciation right. Then I felt guilty for it, for trying to be somebody who I was not.

Life has been too easy for Matt, I think. He grew up comfortably in Fargo, North Dakota, in a homogeneous community blanketed by religion and guided by tradition. Sometimes I worry that when he looks at me, all he sees is a woman washed over and scrubbed clean with an Ivy League education; he doesn't get how rough things are underneath. And that's what I fear most: that he never will. Instead, he'll come to see me simply in terms of my domestic duties: a rosy-cheeked wife, a loving mother, a sheepherder for his kids.

When we were dating, Matt confessed that he wanted to have six kids and a golden retriever, because he grew up with five siblings on their farm in Fargo, along with a golden retriever named Tootsie.

"You'll need two wives then," I said, because all I could think about was my body stretching like that rubbery doll I had as a child, the one whose body became so distorted that she never snapped back into shape.

Matt laughed. "One of these days, you may want six kids, too," he said. I argued with him, but not much. *Maybe he's right,* I thought. Maybe one day I would change, as some of my married friends changed after becoming pregnant.

Still, I couldn't help thinking that Matt had already imagined a role for his future wife, and I worried that no matter how much I wanted the part, I wouldn't always perform well in it. But I also knew that when I was with Matt, nothing else existed for me but him. And now, I am willing to try anything, maybe even suburbia, to make our relationship work.

* * *

We've been engaged for six months, with five left to go, and we have yet to agree on the house. I mark our wedding day's approach with each passing season: we glowed through last summer's engagement, eager to share every last wedding detail with anybody who would listen, and then calmed in the fall. During those first few months, I didn't think much about what it meant to become a wife. Like most brides I know, I immersed myself in cake tastings, dress shopping, and trying to decide whether to order the main meal as chicken or beef and what to do about the vegetarians. My head throbbed with all of the planning that had to be done. Matt and I stole time for each other during the workweek whenever we could. I'd arrive at the coffee shop first, in jeans and a tired sweater, smelling of the perfume he had bought me for my birthday. And a few minutes later, he'd show up, wearing a dark suit paired with a bright tie, apologizing for that conversation or phone call that held him up, but his warm kiss was worth the wait.

But now, with the onset of the harsh winter winds and a touch of cabin fever, I have begun to obsess about the meaning of "us" and, more importantly, "me." Soon, the snow will melt, and with the soggy, muddy ground will come mosquitoes and spring. When the heat of summer settles in, my new life—our new life—will start.

Before we met, Matt, concerned with his number of ex-girlfriends, asked his priest how he would know when he had found the woman he should marry. "You will never be absolutely sure," the priest said. "At some point, you have to take a leap of faith." When Matt proposed, he took his leap of faith. Then

I squeezed my eyes shut and jumped, too. What I do trust completely is Matt's judgment.

As soon as Matt proposed, I made him walk down to the lake with me so that I could show somebody my new ring. I fought the urge to skip or sing; I felt dizzy and gleeful, as if a Fourth of July sparkler were burning in my chest. On our way to the lake, I saw a woman watering the potted plants that hung from her back porch. I ran up the side of her lawn and stuck my engagement ring in her face. "Look at my ring," I said, making sure it landed right beneath her nose. "We're engaged!" Then I felt stupid, but she laughed and called her husband over.

After they congratulated us, Matt and I returned to his house. He made a toast. We sipped champagne. A few days later, Matt had to leave town for work and asked me to pick up his dry cleaning for him while he was gone. Never before had he asked me to run such a conjugal errand. I didn't mind, but I did begin to wonder whether marriage would absorb my identity like a paper towel does a liquid spill. I decided I needed a layer of protection.

"I'm not changing my last name," I announced when he returned home. He didn't recoil or snap, shudder or clear his throat; in fact, he didn't even blink. So I reconsidered. Did I really want to have to explain my different last name to my children's teachers? I decided to negotiate with him instead.

"I will change my name under three conditions," I said, my eyes fixed on his. I flipped up my thumb, forefinger, and then my middle finger with each demand. "One, I can continue to use my name professionally. Two, you will pay off my student loans. And three, you will always wear your wedding ring." I wiggled my three raised fingers at him to signal I wanted an answer. He looked at me as if I were nuts.

"Sure, whatever you want," he said. He doesn't get worked up over emotional things.

But I do get worked up over emotional things. Before I met Matt, the very thought of marriage sent me into a panic. I couldn't imagine depending on somebody else, putting all of my eggs in one basket for somebody else to carry. I used to think that women who wanted nothing more than to get married were weak or desperate. What's funny is that now, when I'm honest with myself, I will admit that I do have a few rather unromantic reasons for wanting to marry. I live thousands of miles from my family and, as I grow older, I feel more alone. I want to wake with a purpose that goes beyond earning money to pay off debt I accumulated the day before, to have a place in which to invest the restless energy that is piling up inside me.

But I also have good reasons for wanting to marry Matt. Captivated by his playful energy, strong build, and rugged handsome looks, I buzz whenever I'm around him. And I know he will make a good husband. He is kind and affectionate, optimistic and trusting. No matter how many hours he puts in at the office, he still greets me with a smile and a kiss. He's always helpful, willing to pitch in. Shortly after we began dating, he and three of his siblings, whom I barely knew, helped me move into my friend's house. They trailed in and out of my apartment like worker bees flowing from a hive, carrying my boxes, suitcases and a folded-up futon. Sometimes, when I look at him, I want to reach inside him and pull out some of his goodness for myself.

Still, I didn't think I'd marry an idealist like Matt. I thought that if I ever settled down it would be with somebody slightly neurotic, the sort of person who drew into himself and resurfaced only when we were together. He'd have dark hair and brown eyes that deepened in color as he contemplated societal ills for hours. He'd change the lightbulbs and take the garbage out and do half the housework as an intellectual statement that he saw me as his equal. We'd live in a loft in lower Manhattan where we'd hang out with other artists and writers who threw around words like *postmodernism* and struggled to make ends meet.

Matt has blondish brown hair that would curl if it grew beyond its current length and pale blue eyes that I now know are just a shade lighter than a North Dakota summer sky. He believes in the guiding principles that have been set before him, whether by the Bible or the Bar Association. He delivers a hard truth like a punch in the gut, and although sometimes his honesty leaves you winded, at least it's out there for you to deal with. And he's not afraid to assert himself if he thinks he's right, but he's fair-minded and will always listen to your side.

Matt's inner life is more straightforward than mine is; he'll mull something over until he has settled it within himself, but then he'll move on. Worries don't turn to acid in his stomach as they do in mine. He's tied to the Midwest, and even though he left it for San Diego to attend law school and for a time practiced law in Houston, he still returned home to be closer to his family. To him, nothing tastes better for breakfast than a buttered, toasted slice of his mom's home-baked bread. He likes fantasy football. And his hero is his dad.

What do I offer Matt in return? I challenge his ideology. I like to think that I've given him a better understanding of people who did not grow up as securely as he did. Through my eyes, he sees how complex people are, that equality of opportunity doesn't truly exist, and that hard work doesn't always get you where you want to go. He's become more sympathetic to those who life has swallowed up, and he has started questioning who he is and why he believes what he does. His soul, which has always been pure and good, is opening up even more to let new light shine in.

But now, flipping for the hundredth time through the brochure for this house that Matt wants to buy, I find myself wondering: is our love enough of a foundation for a marriage, if our backgrounds and expectations are different? I think about spending thirty years with my feet pressed against a linoleum kitchen floor, having small hands grab at my pant legs, while I hold pots steaming with thick meats high above my children's heads to avoid burning them. I think about timing my day so that I have hot food waiting for Matt when he returns home from work, and, while he eats, controlling those chubby little hands that reach for whatever is before them, like the salt and pepper shakers, shiny silverware, and napkins. That's not what I thought I wanted from life, I tell myself, but, then again, I'd never thought about what role I'd play in a marriage. I've always considered myself to be something of a feminist, but can a true feminist be a good wife, if marriage requires roles? Matt sees roles as specialization of labor, which he says is good for efficiency, but I see them as oppressive and defining, with all other needs put ahead of mine. Can a marriage work without clear roles?

With three sisters and no brothers, I grew up in a home in which labor was not divided by gender. Matt, on the other hand, feels comfortable with certain gender roles. He'd love for me to be a stay-at-home mom, keeping his children and home ordered. "I'll never be like that," I warn Matt. I don't want to stay home just so he can feel good about himself for providing for a family. When we go to Fargo to visit his family, I help his mom clean the kitchen while he goes out to the garage to work with his dad. I think I'd prefer having grease from the tractors stain my hands, rather than grease from the frying pan in which we've cooked dinner. In the kitchen, I feel restless and trapped. Outside, in the fields, I imagine I'd feel the way I do when I go for a run around the lakes on a brisk fall day: powerful and free, and then later, satisfied with the fatigue of well-worked muscles.

Two weeks later, Matt still hasn't given up on the house. I think about its pink puffy couches and its inch-thick-glass tables and its gold sink fixtures, all of which create an illusion, a sort of cocoon that I'm not sure I believe in or could sustain. If we buy it, will I become conservative and judgmental, living in a comfort zone created for me by my husband? In the city, you can disappear, but in the suburbs, you conform. There are few differences between you and your neighbor. Already, I'm fighting to remember who I once was, how I once lived in that shared duplex in Ithaca and had envisioned living in a New York loft with a brooding artist. Will my old self vanish completely soon?

Matt cajoles and persists. "The older houses that are closer to the city are more expensive and require more maintenance," he says. "But I want you to be happy." He gives me some time to think.

"Fine," I say a few days later. "You can buy the house." While I sign for it, too, I think of it as his, because I know I can't afford a house like this.

* * *

Because we've decided not to live together before we're married, I move in first, two months before our wedding, with four bathrooms to myself. I try not to look at the walls, which are covered with expensive, textured wallpaper. Each room has a different wallpaper pattern, all competing equally for my attention: in the foyer, sharp, jagged pink, purple, and yellow lines snake across the wall an inch apart; in the kitchen, pink and purple paint splotches splatter the walls like a canvas at which a paintbrush was shaken. Even the dining set, which we bought with the house, offends me, with its pink and purple checkered chair cushions. The house is bolder than I am. In it I feel like an outsider.

I buy a book on how to clean, which lists the products that I will need to remove hard water stains, clean glass without leaving streaks, and kill the mold growing on our tiled shower wall. With it, I plan a scrub path from one end of our house to the other. During lunch, I corner two coworkers, Bobbie and Mary Beth, both of whom have been married for years. Together we walk through the downtown skyways to Target so that they can recommend which brand-name cleaning products I should put in my shopping cart. "Who buys a book on how to clean?" Bobbie asks Mary Beth, as she drops a green scrub pad into my cart. "Isn't it obvious?" To me, it's not.

I do no decorating in our new house; I don't trust my taste yet, nor do I want to spend my hard-earned money on a medley of candles or beaded table lamps. I have no framed pictures to hang on the hooks left in the walls and no leafy plants to set in the path of the sunlight that comes through the windows. Matt brings over his favorite leather chair and sticks it in the living room so that he has a place to sit when he visits.

"Why don't you put some flowers out?" he suggests, but the remark makes me feel inept. I cook dinner for him, putting two slices of wheat bread in the toaster and then a soy burger in the microwave, which dings after one minute. I pad the sandwich with lettuce and tomato, and then slice it diagonally before sliding it onto a plate, because that is all I can think to do to add a wifely touch to this pitiful meal I am about to serve. I put it in front of him, irritated not only because he assumes it's my job to cook for him but also because I don't know how.

He bites into it. "This is good," he says, but I don't believe him. I have a greasy wok and a charred frying pan, neither of which I use properly. I buy prepackaged frozen foods that end up soupy after the ice edging the meats melts; I can't distinguish between the various spices I see at the grocery store, nor do I understand how they could add enough flavor to what I cook to justify their cost.

While sitting at the kitchen table, I hear something whirring, and I go to the window to see the gardener who Matt has hired pushing a lawn mower across our yard. I resist the urge to open the window and yell, "I don't live here!" Because I do.

ONE

And Two Become One

If ever two were one, then surely we. If ever man
were lov'd by wife, then thee.
—Anne Bradstreet

It's official; I'm a wife. I'm Matt's wife, and that gold band on his finger, which he keeps fiddling with, confirms it.

Together, we stand in the living room of our new home, holding hands. Yesterday, we returned from our two-week honeymoon to find our house a wreck. It looked as if the movers Matt had hired to haul his belongings simply picked up his old house and dumped its contents into our new one. I rest my head on his shoulder.

Before we left, Matt had packed up his house and then taped labels to each piece of furniture and each packed box; he drew a diagram of our new house on yellow legal paper to show where each piece of furniture should go; he wrote out specific instructions for the movers, and he negotiated a price with them. As always, he was efficient and organized, and felt comfortable that with all of his planning the job would succeed.

Several months ago, I had moved in like a tornado. Now,

Matt and I laugh over that day, over how it left my car with a crease the length of a baseball bat in the rear quarter panel. But at the time, neither of us thought it was very funny at all.

At first, I had told Matt that I wasn't to blame for the accident. Most Marches in Minnesota mean snow, big piles of it, which have accumulated over the long winter and only grudgingly give way to spring. To make it easier to unpack the clothes and books I had in my trunk and backseat, I decided to back into our new garage. While in reverse, I felt resistance but assumed my back bumper was pressed up against a snowbank. So I gave my car more gas. Bad idea. I heard the metal mailbox grind against my car and looked into my side mirror just in time to see it crumple like a tin can.

"I don't understand," Matt said when he came over. "How can you back your car into a mailbox that is six inches wide and five feet away from a forty-foot-wide driveway?" Matt successfully parallel parks on the first try. His dad, Clarence, taught him how to drive a tractor at age ten to cut hay. While backing up the tractor so that Clarence could hook the mower to it, Matt had to be precise. A slip of the clutch could have resulted in a crushed or severed arm or leg for his dad.

"I thought it was a snowbank," I said, suddenly defensive.

"If you aren't sure, you should stop, get out, and look," he said. "What if you hit a small child?" He knew he had me there. Whenever he drives too fast, I tell him to think about the child who accidentally rides her tricycle into the street. I simply nodded, not wanting to fight in our new house.

Later that day, Matt bought a new mailbox at Home Depot, which he nailed atop the post without saying much. "You're a good driver," he said upon finishing. He put the hammer back in the garage as I tore up the cardboard box in which the mailbox was packaged before placing it in the recycling bin. "You just have a problem in small spaces." He told me to use my mirrors more. And then he offered to give me lessons.

"I'll be more careful," I said, because I couldn't give him that opening. As it was, if he thought I was weaving, he didn't say anything; he simply put one hand on the steering wheel and helped me drive. But I wasn't sure about how I felt about having somebody holding me accountable.

Then on our wedding day, everything changed. Out of nervousness I forgot my wedding vows while we stood at the altar, and Matt mouthed them to me. As I repeated them after him, I knew that we were okay, that I was okay. I knew he'd always be there supporting me, and I knew I'd always be there supporting him.

Matt grabs one of his boxes. "Let's start unpacking," he says, smiling. As usual, he sounds authoritative. His secret, he has told me, is that he thinks before he speaks and uses direct sentences. When I speak, I start and then stop, and then backtrack before starting again until I get my thoughts together. On days when Matt's impatient, he asks, "What is your point?" But today he's patient with me; he lets me approach my point slowly, from four different angles, until I find the one that makes the most sense to me.

"Let's unload one box at a time. It'll be easier to keep the house clean if we have a place for everything," I say, a tip I learned from my how-to-clean book.

He agrees.

I open a box to unpack it. I stare into it, at the coffee cup with his law school insignia on it, a blue sling with white straps that had held his arm to his chest after shoulder surgery, paper clips, an old silver stapler, and a framed photograph of all of his fraternity brothers. I have no idea where to put any of this stuff; none of it seems to belong in our new house. But I don't want to tell him to throw any of it out, so I stick the entire box in the office closet and go back to the living room to get another one. This one contains letters and photographs and what look to be his old journals. Everybody needs privacy, including your spouse. I know there are parts of Matt's past that he may never share with me. So I give him his personal space by closing this box before going through it and putting it in the office closet, too.

Matt walks by and pinches my waist. "Don't!" I say, because it makes me feel fat. But I smile at him and so he loops one arm around me and cups my back with the open palm of his free hand. "Can't you just say 'I love you'?" I tease, and he tackles me. Although being hit with the weight of his body hurts a little bit, his hands, which are gentle and soft, make it worth it. After a quick hug, he releases me.

"What do you think of this picture?" Matt asks, holding up a framed painting of ships going to harbor. I don't think much of it, but I don't have any pictures of my own, and I know he doesn't like the stark walls.

"It's fine," I say.

"Where should we hang it?"

"I don't care," I say, but I'm pleased that he asked.

Matt works with a sense of urgency, of wanting to get the job done. As we walk through the house, he makes a list of what needs to be fixed. It surprises me that he isn't very handy, that he doesn't have the patience for screws that slip through his fingers and clatter to the floor. So the list he makes is for his dad, Clarence, who grew up poor and learned how to fix things out of necessity. Now Clarence refuses to pay somebody else to do a job he can do. As a college student, when the starter on his brown Oldsmobile went bad during a North Dakota winter, Clarence crawled under the car to remove and then repair it, although it was twenty below zero and the pavement was sheeted with ice and snow.

"We should make a toast to our new home," Matt says, after we've put away all of his boxes and hung his pictures. I nod. He goes down to the lower level of our split-level to retrieve a bottle of wine while I sit down at the dining room table. I can see his couch. It doesn't quite fit against the living room wall, so it pokes about an inch into the doorway.

I had grown used to how I had kept house. I liked the lack of furniture, the way the sun shined in through the windows with nothing to obstruct it. I liked the clean surface lines: the gleam of the kitchen counter, the stark mantel, the dark wood of the empty built-in bookshelf. I liked the emptiness of the closets. I even liked the bare walls.

I feel a touch of guilt at being slightly resentful toward Matt's belongings. These empty spaces, which were supposed to be ours to grow into, are quickly filling up with his past. But the past doesn't disappear when you marry; it stays with you and becomes a part of your future. And I know that our challenge is to build one future from two different pasts. But, like most newlyweds, we've yet to discover what marriage is and what it isn't. I am desperate to establish a foundation of trust, love, and respect that will protect our marriage, as I know that negative feelings during the first year of marriage can affect your future together. I don't want to do or say anything that will jeopardize our marriage. Surprisingly, I feel a little bit nervous. So I smile at Matt, and he smiles back as he uncorks the bottle of red wine. He pours me a glass before pouring one for himself, which he swirls and sniffs.

"To my wife," he says, raising his wineglass.

I look at him, my husband, and clink my glass against his.

TWO

An Introduction to Wallpaper Removal

Love does not consist in gazing at each other, but in looking outward together in the same direction.
−Antoine de Saint-Exupéry

On Saturday morning, the alarm buzzes at six a.m., and, at first, I can't place the noise. Although I don't sleep in excessively late on Saturday mornings, I also don't jar myself out of bed with an alarm clock without a good reason. As Matt showers and dresses, I slumber, wrapped up in our bedsheet, until he flips on the bedroom lights.

"Shall we start working?" Matt asks, my North Dakota farm boy turned high-powered attorney.

Working? At seven a.m. on Saturday morning? On weekends, my family never rose with the sun. We pulled the shades to avoid it. And, when we did rise, my parents took us to the park or let us play outdoors with neighborhood kids. Aside from occasionally making us mow the lawn, they didn't put us to work.

As I watch Matt, I can't help but think: in marriage, no matter how much we resist, do we naturally turn into our parents? And why do we base our expectation of who our spouse should be on who we perceived our parents to be in their marriage? How can what worked for our parents work for us when our lives are so different from theirs and times have changed? In our adolescence, we rebel against our parents. We try to separate ourselves from them. So why then, in marriage, do we try to emulate them?

But I get out of bed. This is Day One of our house-remodeling project, and we've agreed that everything pink or purple, the two colors I hate most, will eventually go. This includes the wallpaper throughout our main level and the bedroom carpeting. And we had decided that our first project would be to remove the silver wallpaper in our master bath that glistens like a disco ball. When I found an extra roll of it in our closet, I actually mistook it for Christmas wrapping paper.

I tell Matt I'm going for a jog around our neighborhood before we begin working. I treasure my Saturday morning runs, which clear my head of the stress I've accumulated over the workweek.

"You said yesterday that we'd spend today working," he says.

I had agreed to spend the day working, but it hadn't occurred to me that he meant we'd have to begin at seven a.m. "Why can't we start at eight?" I ask. Our schedules are open all day long; there is nothing hindering us, no obstacles around which we need to work.

"Because that wasn't the plan," he says.

"What plan?" I ask. "I didn't even know we had one." We stand there staring at each other, knowing we're on the brink of an argument that we're not sure we want or need to have. I don't want to back down; I need to go running because, when I don't, I feel uncomfortable in my body. And I want to go now because

I can never motivate myself to run later in the day when it's hot and my energy is zapped.

He goes into the kitchen to make himself breakfast, and I take that to mean he's acquiesced to my run, so I put on jogging shorts, which I find in a box in the storage room, and a tank top. I say good-bye as I lace up my sneakers and tie my house key to my shoes. He says good-bye back. As I run down the street, my knees tingling from my feet pounding against the cement, I wonder whether Matt will expect me to clear things with him that I routinely did before. Don't most people use weekends to relax? Growing up, Matt returned home from school to find notes his dad had left for him with instructions like "Grind Metal." I hope he doesn't think that's the model we'll follow. Any work I do on a weekend I consider a bonus to Matt, not an obligation. I never took into account that he'd have his own idea as to how we'd spend our weekends. I'd looked at my own thoughts and feelings and assumed they'd be his, too.

I have two newlywed friends, Christina and Brenda, both of whom I have known for years. The three of us have decided that you fall in love with a man who is your opposite and then, in marriage, find yourself completely frustrated by him because he's not like you. In fact, he's so not like you that to get your point across you have to develop a new language based solely on analogies.

Christina, a driven attorney with a blond pixie cut, sympathizes with Matt more than she does me. She actually understands his need to color code his sock drawer and closet. "Being a lawyer is all about efficiency," she says. "Your day is divided into ten-minute increments, for which you have to bill." But what's funny is that her husband, Rob, is a creative artist type who doesn't care about money. And it wasn't until after she married him that she discovered he enjoyed playing computer games. That's how he likes to spend his Saturday afternoons.

I do a three-mile loop, sprinting the last half mile, and return home with sweat rolling off me. While I shower, Matt throws a tarp down on the master bathroom floor and lines up the paint scraper, razor blade, and putty knife on the sink. From the doorway of the bathroom, he watches me dress. We both smile. "What do you want to do about the swans?" Matt asks. He's talking about our gold swan sink and bath fixtures. Water spouts from their beaks.

"Let's leave them," I say. They are gaudy and quirky but also a great topic of conversation when we have visitors. Several friends have even offered to buy them from us.

I'm eager to try my hand at remodeling, although I've heard that removing wallpaper is hard work. Matt, with his busy work schedule, hasn't been home much, and I'm looking forward to the two of us being in the same room.

"Start at the top of that wall and work your way to the bottom," he says as soon as I put on an old food-stained T-shirt and jean shorts. "Work while the water is warm. Don't let it go cold."

"Yes, captain," I say, and he laughs. A good sign. I start perforating and scraping. I don't mind that he takes charge; after all, I don't know the purpose of the tools he's brought up from the storage room, and I need direction on how to start removing the silver wallpaper from my side of the bathroom. Already, Matt has unscrewed the bathroom mirror from the wall and taken down the green window curtains, which he set on our bedroom floor.

Matt works in a cutoff shirt, beneath which I see his arm

muscles flex as he scrapes wallpaper glue off the bathroom ceiling. He puts all of his energy into it, glue dripping down his arm like sap down a tree trunk. I lean over to rub glue from his nose, and he waves away my hand impatiently.

He spots glue to my left and says, "You missed a spot." Matt has energy for both of us, but I wish he'd focus it on himself. I would've seen the spot eventually and fixed it; I don't need him pointing it out.

Ten hours later, we're still working, although it's growing dark out. We've only struck up a few conversations, and now the bathroom seems unbearably quiet. Throughout the day, we put down our scoring tools only twice, once for lunch and once for dinner, and I'm tired and my fingers feel arthritic. "Want to go to the movies?" I ask.

"We're not finished yet," he says, and I don't respond at first. I silently fume. I don't want this house to consume us. I'm not spending the next thirty years handing him nails and screws while he stands on a stepladder, and, with his free hand, grabs for whichever tool he's left lying on a countertop.

"This isn't how I want to spend our time together," I say.

Matt doesn't get angry. Instead, he launches into logical lawyer mode, and I start to feel as if I'm on the witness stand. "What did you think marriage was like?" he asks.

His question surprises me. I really thought marriage would be similar to dating, where Matt and I maintained as much of our independence as possible. "I didn't grow up on a farm," I remind him, and, after today's hard work think I wouldn't have survived if I did.

He puts down his sponge and spray bottle and hugs me. "I'm sorry. I thought this would bring us closer," he says. "I know how much you love to take baths, so I thought we'd start with this room first." And then I get it: he doesn't see strands of soggy wallpaper sticking to his arms or mildewing walls needing repair; he sees us building our future. But I'm not sure that his way of building for our future agrees with mine.

THREE

The Icemaker: Whose Money Is It?

Love is an ocean of emotions, entirely surrounded
by expenses.
–Lord Dewar

I hate spending money. I'll wear six-year-old sweaters with holes at the neck as well as faded, ripped jeans a size too small before I'll buy new clothes. In truth, I'm terrified of going broke, which explains why I reacted as I did when Matt announced that he wanted to buy a professional icemaker that produces fifty pounds of ice daily.

Here's what I don't get: Matt uses a ten-year-old lawn mower with three wheels that he bought for $25, drives a rusting '94 Ford Explorer that he refuses to trade in, and yet thinks this $1,340 icemaker is a good deal. And that doesn't include the cost of cutting up our kitchen to install it.

"You do realize all it does is make ice?" I ask. I'm biased. I don't like ice. I don't like how it bumps into my teeth when I drink or how I nearly choke as one slips down my throat when I try to drink around the floating cubes.

He argues for it: tap water ice is cloudy and tastes funny. Each month, he buys a five-pound bag of clear Northstar ice, which takes up half our freezer. "I don't want to taste ice in my drink," he says, and then adds that purchasing an icemaker would save us money and space.

"It's ice," I say. Before we married, I lived paycheck to paycheck in my friend Keiko's remodeled attic. My little space housed all the furniture I had collected after college: a bed, a futon, and a dresser I picked up off the street on garbage night when I was living in New York City as a graduate student. I ate Ramen noodles or baked beans for dinner, until my salary increased enough that I could comfortably afford to pay my monthly bills, including the payments due on six years' worth of private college loans.

I know that financial stress is a leading cause of divorce in America today. So what is it about money that can make us feel cheap or frivolous, weak or powerful, free or dependent? Of all the joint decisions Matt and I must make, how to spend our money feels the most personal, the most painful, and the most irreconcilable. Do other newlyweds find it difficult to share control of the money, regardless of who earns more? Or do they consider it par for the course, part of playing on the same team?

For Brenda, I know, sharing control of the money is downright frustrating. As a single gal, she was both a spender and a responsible saver. She had a savings account, an IRA and mutual funds, plus enough disposable cash to buy what she wanted for the most part. But Mike, who was divorced, has child support payments with which to contend. And so he came into their marriage with little money and no savings, not even a 401(k) plan.

Before we married, Matt and I never talked about money. And, at least for me, it still feels like a touchy subject. So we bank out of two separate checking accounts, although both are held jointly.

He pays the mortgage and his cell phone bill and for his parking spot at work. I pay for our utilities and our groceries and other random bills, of which we've had many since we started our remodeling project. Lately, I've had little, if any, money left over each month. Asking Matt for money makes me feel inadequate and too dependent on him. I don't like to feel that I don't have control over my expenditures. If a bill comes for this icemaker, I know I would have to ask him for money to pay it.

Meanwhile, Christina returned home from work to find Rob spent more than a hundred dollars on "a gift for us." It was called the Audrey.

"What is 'a gift for us'?" Christina asks me when she comes over to my house to jog after work. "It's not something that I want. It's a gadget. And I hate *gadgets*." Objects that are interesting—not decorative—and serve no purpose amount to clutter, she says. And, like Matt, she doesn't do well with clutter. Everything needs a place. Rob, on the other hand, is the master of clutter, or, as he likes to call it, his *interest*. So shortly after they were married they divided up the house for decorating purposes. She gets the first and second floors, while he gets the basement, where, among other items, he stores boxes of Simpsons action figures and more than six hundred movie videos.

"So what exactly is the Audrey?" I ask her.

"I don't know," she says. "It's like this minicomputer with a Web browser."

That doesn't sound too bad to me, and I tell her so.

"We already have two computers in our house with high-speed Internet," she says impatiently. "But apparently Rob thinks it takes too much effort to walk upstairs or downstairs to use them. So he bought the Audrey for us to keep on our main level. The main level . . ."

Got it. The main level is hers. If the Audrey exists on the main level, Christina needs to find a place for it, somewhere she is comfortable displaying it. She finally told him to keep it in a drawer.

"He spent more than a hundred dollars on it! And then he had the nerve to say it was a bargain because it had originally cost six hundred! If you don't need it, it's not a bargain!" While she tries to remind herself that the money is joint, she can't help but feel Rob's spending is frivolous.

A few weeks after being hooked up, the Audrey began collecting dust, and then one day, it just disappeared. So Christina understands why I'm completely annoyed by this icemaker, especially since our refrigerator came with an in-door ice-dispensing unit.

On a Saturday afternoon Matt takes me to Guyers, an appliance showroom. I don't say much on our drive there, except that I can't believe there's actually a market for residential icemakers. To me, an icemaker is a ninety-nine-cent plastic tray into which you pour tap water. Lee, our middle-aged salesman, ushers us to a back room where we watch perfectly square, perfectly clear ice drop from a top-of-the-line icemaker half the size of a dishwasher.

"See how clear it is," he says, offering us a Styrofoam cup to scoop some up. "That's because it's processed upside down." He shows us how minerals and other impurities wash down the drain before the water is frozen into colorless, odorless ice. I feel like I'm in the *Twilight Zone*. Matt pops a cube in his mouth.

"What do you think?" he asks, and, knowing Matt, he'll keep asking until I agree with him. I think he's being ridiculous, and my crossed arms show him that. Still, I remember what my friend Parker, who always takes Matt's side, said when I complained because Matt spent five hundred dollars to rent a boat on July 4 so that we could water-ski on the St. Croix River: "He works hard for his money. Let him enjoy spending it sometimes."

Parker is right. Matt works very hard and puts in very long hours for every cent he earns, and, since he usually invests wisely, I concede to the icemaker.

"There is nothing you can say to make me think this is a good idea. But, I'm not saying no to you either. It's your money, and you can spend it how you want."

"It's our money," he corrects me. But it's not. It's his money, and what I earn is mine. Matt trusts that next paycheck will come. I see money as finite, and I want to hold on to every penny I have, every penny I earn, because it's mine and it guarantees that I'll eat tomorrow and that I won't be eating Ramen noodles or baked beans. While his paycheck is much larger than mine, it's his. It offers me no assurance.

I try to explain this to him but can't. I feel selfish, unwilling to take a risk. Matt gives while I shut down, and from his expression I see he's hurt.

"Let's talk about this another time," I tell him. But it's not the icemaker we need to talk about. We need to find a balance between financial independence and accountability, between spending and saving, or else resentment will build. In marriage, money is intertwined with love, and I don't want money to win.

FOUR

The Scorekeeper

If you are afraid of loneliness, don't marry.
    —Anton Chekhov

*M*att travels constantly for work. On a cold Monday morning, I rise to see him packing, his brown suitcase flipped open at the foot of the bed. The night before, he asked me when I'd like him to pack, and, as usual, I said in the morning. I'd rather have him than his suitcase in bed with me while I try to doze off at night.

He tosses clothes from his closet shelves into his suitcase, and the bed vibrates slightly when they land. He doesn't think as he packs; it's routine for him now. On weekends, his bathroom toiletries stay in his black leather travel bag, for which he installed a bathroom hook.

As I watch him pack, I wonder how busy, overtired, overworked couples are supposed to find time for each other. I thought marriage would give us more time together, and it has, but not much. There are competing demands for our attention now, like a leaking faucet or an unmade bed or family staying with us for the weekend. In a new marriage, will time spent separately cause you to drift apart before your marriage really has a chance to start?

I know Christina shares my concern. This week she is on her own, too. Rob decided to go to Burning Man, an annual experiment in temporary community and self-reliance in the Nevada desert, with friends of his from college. Prior to his departure, he arranged to meet with a local group of people who had attended Burning Man before to get advice on how to prepare for community living. And Christina worries that these new friends of his, who she doesn't know very well, may have found her uptight compared to their free-spirited selves. She wonders if a week at Burning Man might convince Rob that an alternative lifestyle in the desert is better than raking leaves or folding laundry with her.

And while I don't say this out loud, I think to myself that Christina is uptight. But that's what is so endearing about her; that's what her charm is. There is something slightly amusing about it, something comforting in it. I find it in Matt, too.

This trip to Burning Man is so important to Rob that Christina decides to be supportive of it, although it's incredibly different from any experience that she's ever had, although she finds it threatening because her spirit isn't free like his or his friends'. So I think if she can do it, then so can I. I will be supportive of Matt's life and his time away from me, too.

"Where now?" I ask him, as I lie there in bed, because I don't remember to which city he is traveling. Every week it seems he travels somewhere different to take a deposition or meet a new client. He knows at what time the first flight of the day for each major city he regularly travels to departs from Minneapolis: New York at 7:07 a.m., Washington, D.C. at 7:10 a.m., Dallas at 7:11 a.m., San Francisco at 9:00 a.m.

"Portland," he says, shoving socks behind a sweater. He slips the two hangers on which he has hung his suits through the ring at the top of the fold-out compartment of his suitcase. Then he packs his travel bag last. I hear the zipper run around his suitcase before he stands it up on the floor beside the bed, before he leans over to kiss my cheek good-bye. I throw one tired arm around his neck to pull him closer to me. I don't want to let him go.

I envy Matt. He flies weekly to coastal cities where he takes depositions of CEOs I've seen in *Time,* he sleeps in king-size beds with thick down comforters in hotel rooms with marble baths, and at night he goes out for four-course dinners. As a programmer, I wake to a job that requires me to stay put in a nondescript cubicle for ten hours with a computer that crashes at least three times daily.

"When are you coming home?" I ask Matt. Because I know I won't see him for days, I try to wake myself up to spend a few minutes with him, even though it's 4:30 a.m. I rub sleep out of my eyes. They're sensitive to the light coming from the closet.

"I don't know. I hope on Thursday. Maybe Friday." He packs his laptop, stuffing magazines to read on the plane in the front pocket of his carrying case. And then, once again, he is ready to go.

I knew he traveled before we married, and I didn't think it'd bother me. I like to be alone. I'm not afraid of it; I embrace it. When he's away, I'm like a kid whose parents are out of town. I eat junk food, leave the wrappers and dirty dishes on the coffee table, and watch mindless television like *Elimidate*. I kick off my shoes in the doorway, and I drop my coat on the floor. The day before he returns, I wipe down the coffee table, load the dishwasher, and throw my dirty clothes into the washing machine. He likes things neat, organized. I am chaos.

But lately I'm starting to feel our home is a temporary stopping place for him, as familiar to him as the Minneapolis airport. When Matt travels, our house feels empty without his presence. I miss the noise his busy energy generates as he rustles through drawers or looks for his wallet or organizes a top shelf in a closet, never sitting still. And I'm starting to resent that he's not home to help lug garbage cans to the curb, pick up dry cleaning, or meet whichever repair person is coming this week. I find myself counting the tasks I do around the house: *Laundry, score one for me. Washing the dishes, bump my score up to two.* I compare my score to his: *Raking, score one for Matt and a half point for me because I helped.* And I feel cheated, yet somehow vindicated, by my rising score.

Will our kids know their dad by his 6 p.m. phone call? My mom stayed home while my dad worked. Sitting at the kitchen table, she would show me her hands. "My mother told me, 'You see your age in your hands,'" she said. "Every day, before I go to bed, I wash the dishes piled in the sink. Every morning, I come down to see more dirty dishes in the sink. I ask myself, 'What did I accomplish yesterday? What separates yesterday from today or today from tomorrow?'"

I picture my hands wrinkling while Matt pours wine for clients in San Francisco. I think of that dreaded transition from wife to housewife, where who I am becomes unimportant, as I begin to exist only to assist in the smooth operation of my family. Will I disappear completely?

So I can't help it; a week later, when I wake early one morning to find him packing his bag again, I burst.

"I hate this. You're never home, and I have to do all the work around here while you travel."

He sits down on the bed. "Do you think I like traveling this much?" he asks.

"Yes." I know I'm being a brat. I want to provoke him. When he walks out the door, the house will go still, and right now I can't deal with that silence.

"I live out of a suitcase," he says. "Some nights, we work past midnight. You have no idea how stressful it can be. I'd much rather be here with you."

Then I see it in his eyes: he's exhausted. His wire-rim frames hide bluish circles. He pushes himself every day because he doesn't know how to slow down. There are few people he trusts to do a project as well as he does, and so he doesn't delegate work when he should. He does it himself.

"It's okay to complain sometimes," I say, because I understand where he's coming from, and I need to hear from him that the loneliness isn't only mine.

FIVE

How to Talk to an Alpha Dog

I'm not afraid of storms, for I am learning how to sail my ship.
—Louisa May Alcott

I'm beginning to think that I'm at a serious disadvantage in my marriage being a second-born child. Here's my theory: Firstborns think they will always be the alpha dog, and Matt is the oldest of six. While I prefer not to lead, I don't like to be told what to do either. And although I'm eternally grateful for his ability to run interference between me and the world, I'm beginning to resent his fingers dipping into every bowl. But I don't like to argue, which is why I sometimes tell Matt, "Yeah, yeah, yeah," when I really mean, "No." His persistence tires me.

"If you don't want to do something, say so," he says.

"But if I say so, you argue me into it," I protest.

It's a face-off. Neither of us backs down. I spent my younger years behind an alpha dog, my older sister, and while following her orders felt natural, with Matt, I feel coerced.

"Don't tell me you're going to do something if you're not," he says.

"I don't know if I'm going to do something until I do it," I say.

Firstborns, I've learned, see things as black and white. You may want them to lead you into battle, but you don't want them there while you're licking your wounds and crumpling tissue. They don't have much patience for self-pity, which we middle kids love.

Two weeks ago, fearing we'd never celebrate our first anniversary if we did it ourselves, Matt and I decided to hire contractors to remove the remaining wallpaper in our house, patch the beat-up walls, and then paint. Before the workers could begin, Matt and I had to move all of the bedroom furniture into the living room where they'd cover it with a plastic tarp. Plus, we had to clean.

As you know, when there's work to be done, Matt becomes the taskmaster. He tells me to wipe down the coffee table, and, before I begin, to clean a bathroom drawer. As I toss old lipsticks into a garbage can, he tells me there are still cracker crumbs on the coffee table. He delegates to me constantly, and I find myself parroting his five-year-old niece: "You're not the boss of me."

He's used to working with his dad, I think. Clarence knew what needed to be done and how he wanted to do it. And that was the way you were going to do it. With Clarence, Matt knew, there were no alternatives.

When a friend of Matt's got his truck stuck in the mud into which the hard earth softens each spring, Matt borrowed Clarence's truck to pull him out.

"Don't drive in there forward," Clarence said. "Stay up on the road and use a rope to pull him out."

The rope didn't reach. Matt drove in forward and got the truck stuck. He tried to explain what happened to Clarence. "I just thought . . ."

"Don't think. Just do," Clarence said, because he had already thought this one through. He had told Matt the right way to do it, and Matt hadn't listened. And Matt takes this approach with me.

So how much does birth order affect your relationship? Brenda is a firstborn, too. You wouldn't know it from her calm nature, but, from what she says, you would know it if you lived with her. She's the driver. Like Matt, she gets stressed when tasks aren't done within her time frame. And her husband, Mike, a middle child, is more of a procrastinator than I am. It took him months to drill the holes for the handles in the kitchen cabinets during their remodeling project. Then when he finally did, he didn't move or cover any of the appliances, which would have taken him two minutes. And that meant Brenda spent an hour wiping the sawdust from them after he finished drilling the holes.

Christina and Rob have started a home remodeling project, too. To start the project, Rob walked into their kitchen with a hammer and knocked a hole in the wall. "He could have sprung a leak!" Christina says, because Rob tends not to think about the consequences of his actions, but I know she's happy that he did it. With her cautious nature, her approach would have been to consult ten experts before starting the project. But Rob, who is good at initiating, isn't always good at following through. So Christina took over then. She called the carpenter and the plumber and the bank. And then Rob made sure he was home to let them in.

On Tuesday morning, Matt asks me, "Will you stop at a few carpet stores on your way home from work, pick out carpet samples you like, and get price quotes?"

That to me is not a simple errand. That is a Saturday afternoon. I say, "Yeah," although I don't mean it and know I'll regret having made the promise. It's early, and I don't want to fight, so I convince myself I'll make those stops after work.

By noon, I feel tired, and by 6:30 p.m., not even a Grande Starbucks coffee can lift my sinking eyelids. I want to go home and relax on the sofa. There's mail to sort through and laundry to fold, and, before I know it, I've pulled into our driveway. As I walk into the house, I tell myself I can get the quotes tomorrow night or over the weekend.

Matt returns home from work close to ten p.m., after I've put on my pajamas and stretched out in bed. First thing, he asks, "Did you get the quotes?" He's like that; once he delegates something, he hounds me about it until he knows it's done.

"I'll do it tomorrow," I say, and he sighs impatiently, so I think he's annoyed. I feel guilty. Last Saturday, he drove to three shops to compare tile costs.

"I'm not like you," I say. "You know how tired I get." My body crashes more quickly and easily than his does.

"I understand, it's just that you said you'd do it today," he says.

I'm annoyed he still doesn't get sometimes how I operate. He assumes he's right while I stop, think, and analyze. "What difference does it make?" I say.

"You said you would do it."

"You made me say I would do it."

That's it; we can't take it anymore. He goes downstairs to our family room to watch *SportsCenter,* while I struggle to read a chapter of a book and then try to fall asleep, but I can't. I lie there staring up at the ceiling, listening for Matt's footsteps, hoping he'll come upstairs soon.

My mom used to say that whatever attracts you to a man is what will drive you nuts about him in the end. And it's true: Brenda fell in love with Mike because of his easy nature and sense of humor, but now she finds his lackadaisical approach to household chores and finances and remodeling downright frustrating because she feels like everything falls on her shoulders. And I fell in love with Matt because of his drive, but now I find his energy tiring. I know how easy and how dangerous it is for a newlywed to forget what attracted her to her husband in the first place. So, lying there in bed, I try to see things from Matt's point of view and remind myself of his good qualities.

In marriage, can there ever be a winner in an argument, or must you always compromise? There is little satisfaction in compromising. But you have to give to get, to work toward a solution, not a winner.

I can understand why I frustrate him. I operate at a lower energy level than he does. Every day, I experience a two-hour burst of energy, after which I crash. But is it fair for me to sit on the couch watching television while he's still at the office? We both benefit from his labor. And, when he is home, do I want him folding laundry, or do I want him spending quality time with me?

Yet, he sets his life up to be as busy as it is, I think. Why should I have to change my life, washing twice as much laundry and twice as many dishes, to compensate for his lack of time?

There needs to be a balance between his needs and mine, I realize. Does he really operate at a much higher energy level than I do, or does he push himself like his dad, refusing to acknowledge his fatigue?

I think back to how he's pushed us in our remodeling. Our master bathroom is where I retreat to after a long, stressful day. I love to soak in the warm bathwater while flipping through whatever magazine arrived in the mail that day. The dark red paint we used on the bathroom walls feels so warm and inviting, unlike the silver tinfoil-like wallpaper. And it wouldn't have occurred to me to paint our concrete garage floor, but every time I step out of my car onto its shiny gray surface, I feel relaxed and at home. There's no clutter to distract me, no spiderwebs dangling from above to catch in my hair.

His desire to constantly improve our lives is a trait I don't want to take out of him. But if I keep reacting to him, I may do that. While I don't want to end up feeling like his servant, modifying my behaviors to please him, I do need to figure out how to give more of myself to this relationship.

It's lonely lying in bed alone. The bed lacks the warmth his body provides. Finally, I decide to take responsibility for the outcome of this argument, knowing that a solution to our differences is more important than who is right. I put aside my pride and go downstairs to our family room, where Matt's sitting in a black leather chair with the remote control in his hand. He looks up when I enter.

"Next time, I'll say no," I say. I'm not ready to go further than this yet.

"Next time, I'll listen," he says. He clicks the red button on the remote control, and the television screen goes black.

We go upstairs and crawl into bed, and he holds me tight like a football tucked beneath his arm as he charges for the end zone.

SIX

Married and Home on a Friday Night

Marriage is the perfection which love aimed at,
ignorant of what it sought.
−Ralph Waldo Emerson

This isn't how I want to spend Friday night. On our bedroom floor are twelve carpet samples I've laid out like a patchwork quilt. I'm standing on a wool one, wiggling my bare toes against it, waiting for Matt to return home from the office. Tonight, he wants to choose a carpet to replace the faded pink one we inherited when we bought our house.

Earlier, I suggested we go to the movies and fill ourselves with Coke and malt balls and buttery popcorn, but Matt objected. He wants to be able to order the carpet on Monday, and he has to work most of the weekend. But, for a month now, we've spent most of our free time lugging paint cans to the Home Depot counter or debating which dishwasher features would work best for us. Before we married, I knew that you built your home through daily acts, like vacuuming and doing laundry and raking leaves. But what I didn't quite get was how quickly these daily acts would become mundane or how much of your time together they would consume. Every morning, you wake to the same sounds: the buzz of the alarm clock, the hum of the shower, water splashing from the faucet as your husband brushes his teeth. And you wake to the same sights: the momentary thrill of seeing your husband's bare chest as he emerges from the bathroom, his bottom half wrapped in a towel; your husband carefully selects which tie best matches his suit; your side of the bed lifting slightly as he sits on the opposite edge of it to put on his socks and then his shoes. As you settle into this routine, you wonder what happened to passion, when he couldn't sit on a bed next to you without allowing his hands to explore your body before he got up. And it makes you wonder if he is still attracted to you, but you don't want to pester him with your insecurities, so you stare up at the ceiling instead.

Matt equates nurturance with romance, like coming home to a hot meal that I serve. He rubs butter into his potatoes and salts them before eating them. "This is delicious," he says, satisfied. While I take pride in his enjoyment of a meal I've made, I require more intimacy from him.

As a child, I watched my mom stand over a hot stove browning a thick piece of meat and boiling potatoes so that my dad would have a hot plate ready for him shortly after he walked through the back door at five p.m., the ghost catcher, which hung above it, jingling as the door swept through its chimes to announce his arrival. I didn't want to marry because I didn't want to play what I saw as her supporting role. I didn't want to create a comfort zone for my husband to whom I was invisible, faceless and shapeless behind an apron.

Already, though, I am becoming less of an adventurer, more bound to our home. I find the work I put into my marriage, as well as the stability it provides, more rewarding than spending ten hours each day in a cubicle dealing with coworkers who frustrate me. I love responding to Matt's hello, which I hear from wherever I am in the house, upon his arrival home. But I feel as if I'm trying to squeeze into a domesticity role into which I don't quite fit. And I don't want the woman behind the apron, which is still stiff from its packaging, to be forgotten or ignored. What's hard for me is that to feel attractive and confident, I'm finding myself increasingly dependent on Matt's affections. Sweaty with a dirt-streaked face, I feel about as desirable to him as the Home Depot tool clerk in her bright orange smock.

As for Christina, Rob is more romantic than she is. Like Matt, she is functional. She doesn't need twelve long-stem roses or a candlelit dinner or a walk along a moonlit beach to feel romance. What she needs is simple, but it's what Rob finds hardest to give, and that is compliments. She wants to hear him say, "You're beautiful" or "I love you." She needs that verbal reassurance that he sees the good in their relationship, that he is still attracted to her. But Rob finds it difficult to express himself that way. He believes that actions speak louder than words and would rather show his love by leaving rose petals on the bed or buying her a gift certificate for a massage. If she asks him, *Do you love me? Do you think I'm beautiful?* he'll respond in the affirmative, but the compliment itself will not fall from his lips. And so she'll cajole him, begging him to just fake it, and then argue with him, asking why he can't compliment her, until he does so uncomfortably and sarcastically.

"I actually e-mailed him a bunch of different lines that I found on the Internet that he could say to me," she confesses, her fair skin coloring slightly. "I don't care if he means them or not. I'm a sucker; I want to believe him, so I will." Matt, I must say, generously compliments me. He tells me that I look beautiful when I step from the shower or after I apply makeup and fix my hair.

But still, I understand Christina's need for what she defines as romance. Because what I don't get from Matt are blocks of romantic time.

At four p.m., the phone rings. It's Matt, and he wants me to join him for a last-minute happy hour in which he plans to introduce two single friends. "We won't have to stay too long," he says, so I tell him I'd rather stay home. There's no point sitting in traffic and paying for parking downtown for thirty minutes at the bar. I go into the kitchen to make myself a sandwich.

By nine p.m., Matt is still not home. Watching television downstairs, I wait for his truck headlights to roll up over the wall, signaling he has turned into our driveway. I listen for the garage door to open. Matt knows I've been home waiting for him but has chosen to stay out, I fume. He still thinks in bachelor mode; he doesn't think in terms of us.

I can't take it anymore. I grab my jacket and car keys and drive myself to the movie theater where I buy one ticket. Minutes before midnight I return home to a dark house and start to cry. I can hardly hear Matt's voice mail message saying he's sorry he's running late and to come meet him downtown. I delete it before it finishes and crawl into bed.

His key in the door wakes me, but I feign sleep as he shakes me and kisses my cheek. While he undresses in the dark, I lie on my side with my eyes open, staring at the wall. When he crawls beneath the covers, I don't sidle up to him as I usually do. In the morning, the rising sun peeks between the wood blinds and wakes him. He rolls over and says, "I'm sorry I stayed out so late."

"If you were really sorry, you wouldn't have done it." I'm up now as well and have resumed staring at the wall. I don't get out of bed. I'm hurt and angry but need to feel him near me and won't if I come out from beneath our shared comforter.

He pulls my body to his as he tries to explain: They ordered wings and a beer, and then more coworkers showed up, so he drank another beer with them. Before he realized it, it got late.

I stop him from talking. "It seems like whenever you want to have fun, you do it with somebody else." I wait breathless for his response.

"I'm sorry," he says, and says no more, just quietly holds me. I realize if I need romance in our relationship, then, like any illusion, I need to create it. His strengths in our marriage lay elsewhere. I uncoil my body and turn over, rolling into his warm arms. We say nothing more. I feel love, not an illusion of it, but of the sort that gets tested in adversity and strengthens with the passage of time. And I can't imagine life without Matt.

The following Friday, he calls to tell me he'll be home at seven p.m. I peel and start boiling potatoes and set all of the ingredients I'll need to make them buttery and garlicky on the counter. I unwrap the beef tenderloin from its packaging. In our basement I find a bottle of red wine. I set that on our dining room table, along with two large-bowled wineglasses with slightly flared rims, and our wedding china. In a kitchen drawer I tuck my Williams-Sonoma apron and then after a quick shower put on a red spaghetti-strap dress. I blow-dry my hair before curling it, and then sling pearls around my neck. I turn off all the lights in the house and use flickering candles on our glass dining room table as well as on the black slate steps we have in the foyer.

I hear the garage door open. Then Matt enters the foyer. As he studies me, I feel a little ridiculous, unnatural, like I still have rollers left in my hair. But then he grins like he's just picked the forbidden fruit. "This is certainly a surprise," he says, and I grin, too. I feel loved and appreciated, elegant and desired. I feel romance.

SEVEN

The Clothes Horse

Clothes and manners do not make the man; but,
when he is made, they greatly improve his
appearance.
—Henry Ward Beecher

Does this match?" I hear the voice but can't place it until the question is repeated. "Well, does it match?" I roll over, taking my half of the comforter with me. Matt's standing in front of his closet holding what looks to be a tie up to a shirt that's still on its hanger. Without my contacts in, anything past the foot of our bed is a blur. At 4:30 a.m., with my eyes filled with sleep, so are the things right in front of my face, which is where Matt has put both articles of clothing to get my opinion. At this hour, I wouldn't care if I woke to find him wearing polka-dot pants and a cowboy hat, but I blink twice to try to clear my eyes of sleep. I know he'll pester me until I give him an answer.

"I wonder what Michael would think," he says. Michael, a thirty-nine-year-old partner at Matt's law firm, is known around the office as the final arbiter of sartorial standards. Stop in his office, and he'll give you a helpful answer to whatever legal question you've asked as well as a friendly, and often unsolicited, critique of your suit and tie. He believes that people have a social responsibility to raise the level of aesthetic pleasure for those around them. While he is typically easygoing, he has no patience for people who dress inappropriately.

Six years ago, Matt interviewed with Michael. "Most men in Minnesota dress like circus clowns," Michael said to Matt, because he regularly sees men wearing khakis in the dead of winter. From Matt's countenance, Michael thought Matt felt snubbed. "I'm not talking about you," he said. "I'm sure you only wear khakis in the summer."

"No, it's okay," Matt said. "I want to learn." Michael looked at him. He could tell Matt honestly wanted to learn how to dress well but had a long way to go. And so, right there, during Matt's interview, his clothing lessons began. Matt, in a double-breasted suit, with a button-down shirt collar, failed Michael's first test. His suit required a more formal shirt. "Purists would say you shouldn't even wear a tie with a button-down shirt," Michael said.

After Matt began working as an associate, Michael stopped by his office periodically to comment on his progress, criticizing him for wearing plain white cotton T-shirts beneath casual, long-sleeved shirts, and to praise him. As Matt's training became more advanced, Michael explained the importance of fabric weight and texture.

And these are the lessons that Matt tries to pass on to me as I dress for work in the morning, lazily scanning my closet for a sweater to wear with my jeans. I'm amused that he asks for my advice on clothes. Unlike many women, I have never taken much of an interest in clothes and generally choose comfort over style. When we were dating, my outfits often appalled Matt, who rarely left the house in sneakers, unless on his way to exercise. I dressed in thick, baggy sweaters to avoid feeling drafts against my bare skin. Beneath dress pants I wore tube socks I've had since high school. I refused to buy clothes labeled Dry Clean, as I'd spend more getting the clothes cleaned than I did to purchase them. Whenever I went over to Matt's house, he'd grab his sticky brush and roll it over me to remove lint and strands of my hair from my sweaters.

"You need new clothes," he said, after I showed up at his house in one of my favorite sweaters. It was dark gray and had frizzed from years of being yanked around by the agitator in washing machines. But it was comfortable and warm.

"Not everybody has the money to dress as well as you do," I said. Matt wrote out a check to me for more than my weekly salary and left it for me on his kitchen counter. For days, it sat there, his signature scribbled like chicken scratch at the bottom of it, while I debated whether to cash it.

When Matt and I met, he had a mental image of the woman he would marry. She'd have long, curly hair, work as a teacher or a nurse, enjoy keeping house, and want six children. My hair falls flat against my back, I want two or three kids at the most, and I used toilet bowl cleaner on our glass table because I thought all cleaning products were essentially the same, just marketed differently.

I refused to change even one bit to fit his image. He would love me for who I was, or I wouldn't let him love me at all. Beauty fades, I told myself. My soul, my very being, should be enough to attract Matt to me. A physical attraction held at a feverous pitch may carry us to the altar, but it wouldn't sustain a marriage. But still, I did wonder how desirable I was when I walked through his house in sweatpants, and even my nice clothes had holes in them.

"Cash the check," said Bobbie, my girlfriend at work, and so begrudgingly I finally did. I called my friend, Jennifer, an attorney who flies to New York City to shop and who once bought a cashmere sweater for her baby. She met me at Marshall Field's, where she ushered me into a dressing room and started throwing clothes over the door for me to try on. I tried not to look at the price tags.

I took my clothes to the cashier, and, as she removed their security tags, I felt guilty, almost sick, over the amount I had spent. One of my purchases, black leather boots with a half-inch heel, I wore to a party where I sat too close to a bonfire, causing the leather to melt, fray, and turn white. Because of how much I had paid for them, I refused to throw them out, even though they looked as if I had marched for miles over frozen tundra in them.

Christina has been getting her own fashion lessons from Rob. While she dresses better than I do, her clothes reflect the type of work she does. They are conservative and career-oriented, cream-colored blouses buttoned all of the way up beneath suit jackets, skirts landing beneath the knee. Whenever Rob, who loves to shop, buys her a shirt or a skirt, it ends up being the most hip item in her closet.

But, unlike me, it's not that Christina doesn't care for clothes; it's that she doesn't like to shop. She is self-conscious about her body and feels uncomfortable in dressing rooms turning in front of a three-way mirror. Trying to find clothes that fit her properly frustrates her. But, after Rob's Burning Man experience, Christina has started feeling insecure about her clothes: Is what she's wearing cool or hip enough for Rob and his friends? So, like me, she has started to make a concerted effort to dress better.

After Matt and I married and moved into our new house, I found a picture of a woman Matt had dated while living in

Texas. I studied her carefully. Her black, curly hair was teased up in front, each cascading ringlet hair-sprayed to perfection. Her long fingernails were painted hot pink. Her black sweater dipped to reveal plump cleavage. She looked exactly as he had described his future wife.

"That look went out in the eighties," I said, passing the picture to him. Why hadn't he married her? I wondered. She obviously took great care in her appearance. I felt frumpy. And so later, when Matt said he thought I should invest in a classic suit, I said okay, even though I wear jeans to work.

At Nordstrom, I dug out a leather patchwork skirt from a sale rack. Matt rolled his eyes. He insisted the salesperson help us, and she brought me conservative suits I immediately disliked but felt obligated to try on. I pulled my shirt over my head, and my hair frizzed from static. Already, I was annoyed.

I came out and stood in front of the three-way mirror. While the salesperson adjusted the skirt seams, I fussed like a five-year-old girl who doesn't want to wear a white lacy dress.

"I look so old," I complained because of the shoulder pads stitched into the jacket and the thick gold buttons that adorned it. Its price tag dangled from my sleeve. When I turned it over, I saw it cost more than I had spent in the past year on clothes. I insisted we leave without purchasing a thing.

One day, I ran out of clean socks and grabbed a pair of Matt's designer ones from his well-organized drawer. They were a little too big for me. The material that was supposed to cup my heel flopped over the back side of my loafers, but my feet felt wonderfully snug in them. My mom, ever thrifty, used to turn my socks inside out whenever my toes poked out of them, stitch about an inch down from the toe of the sock, before turning them right side out and then cutting off the extra fabric. That left my socks an inch shorter but without holes. With Matt's socks, no seams cut into my toes leaving red lines, and no blisters formed on my heels where the fabric rubbed. I grew addicted to the comfort they provided.

"You must stop stealing my socks," Matt said, because it had become a daily event for me now, and he had no clean ones left in his drawer. I was too cheap to buy my own socks, so he finally went out and bought me a pair. My feet felt perfectly snug in these, too, even my heel, which gently rested on the heel seam. Days later, I went out and bought several new pairs of silk, wool, and cotton socks, all in my own size. I was ready to graduate to real clothes.

A few weeks later, when we were vacationing in Colorado, Matt and I found a shop with clothes marked over half off due to the downturn in the economy and the ending tourist season. He liked the styles, I liked the prices, and we left with five new outfits for me. I wore them to work one after another.

"Did Matt buy those for you?" Bobbie asked, because even my cream-colored socks matched my cream-colored pants. It was obvious he had.

When I walk into stores wearing my new clothes, salespeople approach me and ask if I need help. And while I didn't realize it before, I had felt hurt when salespeople ignored me. I assumed it was because they knew I couldn't afford the clothes. And that created self-doubt within me and lowered my self-esteem. Without self-confidence in your body image, you will find it difficult to maintain a relationship. Like Michael, I enjoy the attention and respect I get from being well dressed, and I'm starting to overcome my social insecurities.

Admiring my newfound style, Matt decided he needed to buy a tailored navy blue suit to wear during an upcoming trial. Matt is a careful shopper. When he finds something that he likes, he compares it to other versions to figure out what's the best buy for his money. I don't have that kind of patience. I think either you like it or you don't, either you can afford it or you can't, and, if you can't afford it, why look for something else you may not like as much? Just put it back, and eventually you will find something within your budget that you do like. And so when we shop together, I get frustrated and bored.

We went to the first floor of Nordstrom where he asked for the salesperson he always uses and whose judgment he trusts. Together they looked through the endless rows of jackets to find the one that hung just right. In the dressing room, the tailor pinned Matt's pant leg, as I gazed at his mirrored reflection. There he stood, broad-shouldered and commanding. Around his neck, he roped a yellow tie and then knotted it. Suddenly, I was awakened.

"After this, let's go home," I whispered in his ear. I finally understood the power of dress. Outward appearances do stir desires, like shiny paper and ribbon that wrap a gift. You may not keep your attraction at the same feverous pitch you did while dating, but you should still fan the flames of desire once in a while. Because you never know where the resulting sparks may lead.

EIGHT

Dealing with Temptation

Better shun the bait than struggle in the snare.
–John Dryden

A new blond has joined my adult recreational soccer team. Tabloid pretty, she is single, tall and thin with bright blue eyes. She makes wisecracks, and all of the guys flirt with her. "What are you doing tonight?" they ask her, a question most men don't ask me anymore. As I watch her from the sidelines, I realize that I have been removed from that pool of single women, have lost possibilities. I am, so to speak, the old married woman. I feel undesirable. Worse, I watch my ex-flirtation, Nick, flirt with her, and I begin to feel invisible.

Back when Matt and I were dating, Nick and I met on the soccer field as we waited for the kickoff. He introduced himself and I shook his hand, and from the expression on my face I'm sure he knew that I was attracted to him. He had black curly hair and olive skin, with hazel eyes that made me blush and then giggle. I'm sure I even stammered. But, after that first game, my shyness disappeared, and I flirted with him like mad.

At five foot ten, he isn't much taller than I am, but he makes up for his lack of height in other ways. Before our games, I would watch his uniform slide over his taut stomach as he changed shirts. I admired how he used his body to shield the ball from his opponents and his skill in dribbling past them. After our games, I somehow always managed to get a seat next to him at the bar, though I was never quite sure whether this was by his design or mine. But I got jittery whenever our hands touched when we reached for the same basket of popcorn or we bumped knees under the table.

Even then I knew that my connection to him didn't go beyond the physical. I didn't have a longing to share things with him, as I did with Matt. He didn't have Matt's optimism or authoritativeness or gregariousness. But what Nick did have was a tattoo of an anchor on his bicep, only half of which I could see beneath his soccer shirt, and a physical presence that I felt whenever he was in the vicinity.

Meanwhile, I was falling in love with Matt, but trying to get closer to him was painful. The more of myself I put out there, the more I lost. He was trying to sort out whether he wanted to marry me, and his ambivalence hurt. It cheated me out of what I wanted most: that certainty that we belonged together, that assurance that if we did marry, it would be forever, because we couldn't imagine life without each other. How could I be sure that he was the one when he had so many doubts about me? And, after being together for more than a year, why hadn't we come together naturally? With Nick, I didn't have to compete for his attention with his friends or his job or his family; in that hour at the bar, I was it. I could flirt with him as much or as little as I liked and still get that adrenaline rush from it. Plus, there was no heartbreak associated with it, no risk. I never knew if Nick really liked me, nor did I want to know or care. Not knowing meant

I could pretend that he did like me, without having to act on it. I could be reckless without the responsibility.

One Friday night, Matt and I had plans to go to dinner. He had promised to come over early to help me change my flat tire. But around noon, he called to say his friends were heading to a bar later that afternoon and he wanted to join them. "I want you to come, too," he said, and I could tell he meant it. "We can change your tire tomorrow morning." I didn't want to go. I was beginning to feel like an afterthought, a third wheel, a postscript to the brief that was due or the relative who was coming into town or the last-minute happy hour one of his friends had decided to put on.

So when Matt asked me to join him and his friends at the bar, I snapped. "You go," I said, and hung up. I was done battling him for time for us. I had been in serious relationships before, and I knew the routine. You come up with all kinds of reasons as to why your relationship isn't progressing to the next level: you don't have enough money to get married; you want to be more stable in your career first; you need just a little more time to think. But often the truth is simpler than that. You just aren't right for each other. In my early twenties, I spent four years hanging onto a relationship that in my heart I knew was going nowhere. I held on out of both guilt and fear: guilt that I didn't love him as he did me, and fear that if I gave him up I'd end up alone. When that relationship finally ended, I promised myself that from then on I'd call a spade a spade. And it was plain to see that my relationship with Matt was going nowhere.

So I called up Nick and asked *him* to come over to help me change my tire. Before he arrived, I cleaned my bedroom. I folded all of my clean clothes and put what was dirty in my hamper. I made my bed, pulling my comforter over my pillows, which I even fluffed. Then I darkened my lashes with two coats of mascara and lined my eyes with black pencil. As I stared back at my reflection, I thought, *What am I doing?* But it was too late to give myself an answer. I heard Nick's car pull up and from my bedroom window saw him get out of his car with a jack.

I met him at the door. It was odd seeing him outside of soccer and the neighborhood bar; it was even odder seeing him in street clothes. Suddenly, he became less of a fantasy and more real. We talked. As he propped up my car and put on my spare, he told me where he'd be later that night. And then he left.

I took a walk around the lake then. It was hot out. The sun was so bright that on certain parts of the path I had to squint or use my hand to shield my eyes. I needed time to think. Should I meet Nick? What did I want?

When I returned home from my walk, I found a dozen roses on my bed. They were from Matt. On the card, he had written that he was sorry about dinner and that he loved me. For a moment, I felt like a cheater, a schmuck. Then I felt angry; I hated that I had to push him this far before he'd respond to my needs. And I didn't trust that his apology meant that he would put me first in his life. I took it to mean that he didn't want me angry with him because it made him feel guilty. So I chucked the roses in the garbage.

I never met Nick out that night. Nor did I answer my phone when Matt called. In two weeks, I was heading to Russia for a six-week summer study program, for which I had secured a leave of absence from work. And Matt was flying over there with me. We were planning to tour Moscow and St. Petersburg before he left and I began my course. With that in mind, I wasn't ready to springboard into a relationship, however minor, with Nick.

Before we left for Russia, Matt and I patched things up, but our relationship wasn't the same. I didn't feel the same enthusiasm upon hearing his voice when he left a voice mail for me.

I didn't feel the same enthusiasm when I saw his Ford Explorer pull up in front of my house. But by the end of our two-week tour of Russia, something in both of us had changed. I felt it early one morning while we were sitting on a cast-iron park bench. The grass around us was still wet with dew. Matt scribbled notes in his journal while I fed bread crumbs to the pigeons flocked at our feet. And then he looked at me almost as if he never had seen me before. It made me feel like the sunlight hit me and only me. I felt like the star in one of those stupid shampoo commercials. He smiled, and I leaned over and rubbed his head.

"What are you writing?" I asked.

"Nothing," he said. "But you have to promise me that you won't read what I've written."

I promised, but I didn't need to read his journal. I knew what he had written. And four weeks later when I returned home, I saw that I was right: there, on his dining room table, was a bottle of chilled Dom Perignon champagne and a box that held another box that held another box that held my ring.

I didn't see Nick much during my engagement period. He had taken a new job, and I had cut back on soccer to keep up with the demands of wedding planning. And whenever I did see him, I couldn't find a way to tell him that I was engaged, although I'm sure he knew. I even hid my hand on which Matt had slid the engagement ring. Around him, that ring, which I proudly showed off to store clerks and gas station attendants, made me feel as if I had gained twenty pounds or got a bad haircut.

Now, as I watch Nick talking with the new blond, I realize that this is the first time I've seen him since my wedding. I don't approach him. My attraction to him, which hasn't disappeared with marriage, feels like a betrayal of Matt. And that instant gratification that I got from Nick, that momentary escape from loneliness that comes from when another pair of eyes turn on you, can no longer be a part of the solution to problems that Matt and I may have in our marriage. I can't splinter our intimacy by relying on temporary fixes, on adrenaline rushes to get me through our lows. I have to ask for and get what I need from my husband. For your love to stand the test of time, you must commit to behaviors that protect your marriage, in spite of how you feel about your spouse on that particular day. And while it's not hard to let go of Nick, it is hard to let go of the idea of him, of having an outlet, of having another way of securing yourself.

When Nick finishes his conversation with the blond, he sees me and comes over. "Congratulations," he says.

"Thank you," I say, and slowly I raise my left hand. That band symbolizes part of who I am now. And even though I still don't know exactly who that person is, I do know that Matt is a part of her new identity.

NINE

Warts and Other Character Flaws

*The supreme happiness of life is the conviction of
being loved for yourself, or more correctly, being
loved in spite of yourself.*

–Victor Hugo

You have the proclivities of a twelve-year-old girl," Matt says, laughing, and I have to look up the word to fully understand its meaning. *Proclivity: an inclination or predisposition toward something.* I get it. He's making fun of my *Cosmo* magazine subscription.

What do you do about quirks that drive you nuts, those little behaviors or warts that are a part of the person you love? And what do you do about your own warts? My ponderings about warts started as Matt and I were driving to Fargo to visit his parents. It takes three hours to get there from Minneapolis. Matt drove while holding my hand. He had the station tuned to classical music on NPR. Sleepy-eyed, I stared out the window at the flat prairie, reading the car dealership and pro-life and hotel billboards that we passed. When we lost the signal, Matt hit the Scan button. It landed on a pop radio station. Without thinking, I started to rap along with Eminem, bopping my head like a chicken pecking at feed. I knew all of the words. And I even knew some of the hand signals from his *Slim Shady* video. "How do you know this song?" he asked in disbelief.

"I just do," I said sheepishly. I have to admit it: I'm a pop culture addict. While I try to minimize the time I spend on the couch in front of the television, every now and then I'll get snagged by an *E! True Hollywood Story*.

Matt thinks all blond pop stars, from Jessica Simpson to Christina Aguilera, are Britney Spears. He doesn't know that J Lo married Marc Anthony, nor does he know (or care) that she's been married twice before. He has no idea who Ashton Kutcher is or that he is dating Demi Moore. And he has never watched a full hour of reality TV, except for one episode of the first *The Bachelorette,* but I suspect that was only because he was smitten with Trista.

But my biggest pop culture addiction is *Cosmo* magazine. When we were dating, Matt saw an issue of it on my coffee table. "It's my roommate's magazine," I explained, posing as the intellectual. The address label on the back proved it was hers. And on the back of the *Atlantic Monthly,* a magazine to which Matt also subscribed, was an address label with my name printed on it. But what I didn't tell Matt was that I faithfully read *Cosmo* first, and had actually put some of its advice into practice.

Matt knows the names of the battleships from World Wars I and II like I know the names of the *American Idol* finalists. He recognizes senators and judges and presidential hopefuls like I recognize the cast members from *The OC.* He gets his statistics from the *Wall Street Journal*; I get mine from *Cosmo.* So during our first two months of marriage, I resisted subscribing to *Cosmo* and exposing myself to him as a pop culture junkie. Then *CosmoGIRL* started arriving in my mailbox. I was certain my ex-roommate, who knew my secret, had bought me a subscription as a joke. I applauded myself for being able to toss that one, with its advice on how to be popular or snag a date for prom night, straight into the trash.

Then finally I gave in while standing in the checkout line at the supermarket. I bought an issue of *Cosmo* and tore the subscription card from it. Six weeks later, my first issue arrived. It turned a bad day good. While Matt sat in our formal living room reading the *New York Times* beneath the lamplight, I headed straight for my bathtub, where I soaked for a half hour while thumbing through *Cosmo*.

Like a trashy romance novel, the magazine sucked me in. Its health and beauty tips promised to keep Matt fixated on me for years. To alleviate the boredom that can result from familiarity, I decided to get a makeover every six months. And I'd shed a few pounds and lift weights to help prevent the hard truths of aging or gravity from taking their toll on my body. With *Cosmo*'s flirty moves I could keep the stresses of our daily lives from diminishing the pleasure we find in each other.

A few days later, I went shopping for the tools that I'd need. I bought some liquid eyeliner to try for a smoky, mysterious effect. The line I drew across my eyelid was jagged. When I tried to correct it, it smeared. Then I ate so much from a pan of brownies that I had baked that I had to make a second pan to hide how much I had eaten from the first. So forget the flirty moves. With my eyes looking bruised and a pan of brownies distending my stomach, I was in no mood to show delight when Matt came home from work.

He walked into the kitchen where he found me at the sink. He was still in his suit. I was scrubbing clean the brownie pan, trying to figure out why I had devoured six of them and wondering what made it so difficult for me to be *Cosmo*'s definition of a fearless female. Since Matt and I married, I seemed to be suffering from newlywed 15, where every month my weight crept up by a half pound as I tasted dinner while preparing it. Did the potatoes have enough salt and butter in them? Were the sautéed mushrooms tender? Was the sirloin steak drying out in the broiler? When I was single, I ate one cup of instant oatmeal for any meal that I did not eat out. And I exercised more than I did laundry.

On the kitchen counter was the latest issue of *Cosmo*. "Big sex news?" Matt said, reading a headline from the cover. He flipped through the magazine, shaking his head at all of the advertisements for shoes and clothes and makeup, and then put it down.

Then I felt silly. What will sustain our marriage is a deep friendship, not a flat stomach or smooth skin or highlights.

That night, I couldn't find my *Cosmo* magazine. "Have you seen it?" I asked Matt. He said he hadn't. But then I found it on his nightstand, propped open to the big sex news. In that moment, I knew he had grown to accept that little wart I had tried to hide from him, and I no longer felt pressured to change.

TEN

Trust and a Black Lace Blouse

All jealousy must be strangled in its birth,
or time will soon make it strong enough to
overcome the truth.
—Sir William D'Avenant

At a party one weekend, I looked up from a glass of white wine to see Matt talking to a pretty brunette in a black lace blouse. She stood at his elbow, her eyes alive, a smile tugging at her lips. Because loud music blared from the stereo, Matt leaned over to speak directly into her ear. She laughed and clapped her hands and flung her hair back. My eyes locked on her, on him, on their proximity to each other.

Matt and I had parted after removing our shoes at the door. That was a big step for me; usually, I cling to him like a two-year-old to her parent as he works the room like a politician, shaking hands with people he barely knows. I saw my friend, Amanda, and together we headed for the hors d'oeuvres table, where we loaded our paper plates with mini-quiches, crackers, and cheeses. We talked for a while. She told me about her husband, I told her about my job, and then we each ate one of the warm spinach quiches on our plates. It was then, after I had swallowed the last bit of quiche and had lifted my glass of wine to my lips, that I observed Matt talking to the brunette.

Deluged with memories, I sipped my wine in silence. Three years ago, I met Matt on a blind date. My roommate, Keiko, had set us up. "You're my only single friend he hasn't dated," she said. "You'll go out with him three times and that's it, but you'll have tons of fun." As I didn't know many people in Minneapolis, I struggled to find people to go out with on Saturday nights, and so a blind date—even with a serial dater—sounded appealing.

He picked me up in his maroon Ford Explorer and took me to play tennis. From his black gym bag he retrieved two bottles of Gatorade, a grape and an orange, and set them both down on the tennis court. "Pick your favorite one," he said. *Smooth,* I thought. I chose grape and headed toward my end of the court. I am a competitive person, but he, as a patient one, waited for me to make the mistakes. I got frustrated with our endless volleying and tried slamming balls back at him. My aggressive shots ended up in one of three places: in the net, outside the tennis court, or, rarely, in bounds, scoring a point for me. He easily won the game.

When our game ended, he took me to a nearby Chinese restaurant for dinner. While I fiddled with my fork over dinner, emptying my glass of water before our waiter took our order, Matt talked. Even after his food arrived and sat steaming before him, Matt talked. As he talked, I realized that while I enjoyed his company, we'd never work. Matt's social skills put him outside my comfort zone.

Worse, I learned about a month later, Matt flirted. As we walked the paved path encompassing Lake Harriet, his head swiveled whenever a lanky girl in a bikini top Rollerbladed past.

"Do you ever stop looking at girls?" I asked.

"I thought I knew the guy she was with."

"How is it you know every guy who's with a girl in a bikini?" I asked.

On our next walk, he showed up wearing dark sunglasses that hid his blue eyes.

"If your head moves, I know you're looking," I said. He feigned ignorance. I stopped walking. "I don't care if you look when I'm not around. But don't do it when you're with me, okay? It hurts my feelings." That statement wasn't entirely true: I did care if he looked, but at least if I didn't see it, I could deny it. He obliged.

For three months, we were very happy. He was as daring as a lion tamer. His presence commanded authority as the captain of an army would. I liked his boldness, his honesty, his need for perfection. And he said he liked me for my artistic side, for always trying to do the right thing, for not caring what people thought of me. But then, as our relationship progressed, we began to uncover the bad counterparts of the good character traits we had once seen in each other. I no longer admired his need for perfection; I saw him as inflexible and demanding, while my messy habits and inattention to my physical appearance wore on him. When I left the house on a Saturday afternoon wearing a sweatshirt and sneakers, he no longer credited my unconformity but faulted me for not dressing fashionably instead. At first, I fought for us, but I quickly figured out that it was a battle I'd lose. Our differences had become irreconcilable, and, once again, his eyes had begun to wander.

After six months, we mutually decided to break up while sitting in the front seat of his truck parked outside my house.

"You're shallow," I said angrily. His radio hummed.

"I know," he said. I wasn't sure if he meant it or said it to avoid a fight, but I hadn't the energy to pursue it. We said good-bye there.

"There will always be somebody else," my mom said when I called home, and I knew she was right. Everywhere I looked, I saw single, available men: at the grocery store pushing carts that contained more pop than food, while jogging around the lake early Saturday morning, and even while perusing the travel section of the bookstore.

"Matt's miserable," my roommate, Keiko, said. "He misses you." But I didn't care. His criticism was a turnoff and helped me to move on. But a month later, when I was in Ithaca visiting my parents, I called into my voice mail and heard a message that he had left. He said he knew now what he hadn't before: I was *The One*. At first, I wasn't sure how to respond to him, but after listening to his message twice, I returned his call a day later. We talked for an hour, and, after he listened to what I had to say, he apologized for the pain he had caused me. I was touched.

That Friday night, I had made a date with a tall, attractive guy but I canceled it to give Matt one last try. Slowly, we began dating again. And this time he was different.

At parties, he tightly held my hand and didn't release it until I relaxed. If he saw discomfort on my face, he returned to my side to reassure me that he was there. Yet I couldn't let go of that nagging doubt: had he changed, or had he just changed how he behaved in front of me?

A month ago, I learned that during our break, he had gone out on three dates with a woman he had met through a friend. Even in his misery, he still had the energy to pursue somebody else, I thought. "It meant nothing," he assured me. But to me it meant my mom's axiom still held true: there would always be a new body to turn his head or mine. And so, as he spoke with the brunette at the party, it occurred to me that we wouldn't always know who was passing through each other's lives. All we could do was trust each other, which required vulnerability—a fear of losing the man who I love so much—that I didn't feel ready for. But I knew that this was my problem, not his. I can't base my judgment of Matt on a small snapshot in time. I need to appreciate the changes he's made for me and allow him to grow. Yet I'm always saddened by how easily he can talk to other women. I know that my jealousy is based on fear, not love, and I don't want it to affect our relationship. So I pasted on an unnatural smile that began to make my face ache. Finally I went downstairs to avoid looking at them.

For a moment, I wished I had married a man like my dad. Two introverts in a family of extroverts, we understand each other. Neither of us speak much to people we don't know, and that makes us socially dependent on one another. I craved that same dependency from Matt, thinking it would somehow merge us together so that we couldn't be split apart.

But that's not who Matt is. I married him for his confidence, for his ability to put me at ease, and it isn't fair to expect him to change now because of my insecurities.

Soon after I went downstairs, Matt caught up with me. "Where have you been?" he asked, putting his arm around my waist.

I didn't respond and hugged him instead.

ELEVEN

See Work to Do

Don't judge each day by the harvest you reap,
but by the seeds you plant.
–Robert Louis Stevenson

Three months after our wedding, I wake up in the middle of the night with the sudden realization that Matt and I have made a huge mistake in marrying for one reason: at times I can't stand him. Is it possible to both love and hate somebody at the same time? And I'm confused because some of his behaviors are not what I expected from him, which makes me wonder: does any bride truly know her husband before her wedding day? Or is it only with the passing of time and the challenges that follow that his true character becomes clear to her? Can she know how much some of his character traits will affect her until they become an integral part of her life? Nobody is without his or her flaws. And what at first seems charming, like Matt's need to have everything—toothbrushes, magazines, shoes, silverware—set perfectly straight, can quickly become downright annoying when you're married.

Recently, Christina confided that she was surprised by how

much Rob's free spirit affects her. When she first met him, she had grown weary of the types of men she normally dated: lawyers, accountants, engineers—responsible men who spent Saturday nights balancing their checkbooks and called her when they said they would, which, for her, translated to boring. But Rob, a marketing consultant, was different. He could socialize with anyone, in any situation, and be at ease. He liked traveling, theater, rock concerts, sports, and, most importantly, her girl-friends. She felt freer when she was with him, like she finally un-derstood what stopping to smell the roses really meant. But now she finds that with his free spirit comes different priorities. He will never say no to a friend and will always opt to go out, even if dishes are piling in the sink. All of the household budgeting falls to her. Where his free spirit can free her, it can also trap her, because she ends up doing the dishes that are piled in the sink and paying the bills. And, unlike Rob, she finds it difficult to un-wind until she knows all of the work in the house is done. At first, Rob's ability to relax irritated her. But now she's realizing that her feelings toward him have more to do with her feelings about herself. She deeply envies Rob's ability to relax and enjoy his free time.

"Every Saturday morning, I wake up with a task list in my head. I know exactly what needs to be done around the house. But Rob can sleep until ten a.m., and then he reads the paper when he gets up!" she says agonizingly, and this makes me laugh.

"You're just like Matt," I say, because he is a driver, too. Lately it seems all he and I ever do in our free time is work on our house. No matter what I do, it isn't good enough for Matt. And no matter how good of a job he does, he won't stop working.

After Matt and I spent a beautiful Saturday afternoon clean-ing out our storage room, he decides we should paint our garage floor with a shiny, gray EPOXYShield to cover its aqua antifreeze and dark brown oil stains. First, we move everything that had been sitting on the garage floor to the storage room, including his snowblower and my bike. Then, we sweep the garage floor clean. Clumped in corners we find dead spiders and other bugs, as well as leaves the wind had blown in. I sweep what I can, but finally, the sight of the curled-up bugs catching in my broom is too much. I refuse to bend closer to them to sweep them up into my dustpan, especially the hardened white worms, which crunch when I accidentally step on a pile of them. "Can you finish?" I ask Matt. "These bugs are making me nauseous."

"They're dead bugs," he says. "They can't hurt you." To remove spiderwebs from the windows, he simply reached up and grabbed them, tossing them to the floor. But he grants my request and motions for me to get out of the garage.

When he finishes sweeping the dead bugs into the dustpan, he hoses off the garage floor, sending a dirty stream of water swirling down the driveway and into the gutter, while I stand on our front lawn watching him work. His yellow shorts, wet from the spraying water, cling to his thighs, while mud speckles his forehead. He looks cute.

"Don't stand there," he says, wiping sweat from his brow. "See work to do."

What does that mean? Am I supposed to mow the lawn? Do the dishes? I thought our project was to paint the garage floor, and, as far as I am concerned, my job is over. We have only one paintbrush, and I know Matt won't trust me to lay the first coat. As he pours the two epoxy components into a bucket and starts mixing them together with a stirring stick, I go into the storage room to find something to do. All I find in there are the tools, like screwdrivers and hammers, he has laid out on his workbench, each one of them perfectly aligned, and boxes he has yet to unpack. I could unpack his boxes, I think, but I'm suddenly not sure how he'd feel about me going through his belongings. I see nothing to do, and so I decide to do what he had told me to do in the garage. I decide to sweep.

"What are you doing?" Matt asks. He saw me take the broom from the hook from which it hung in the garage.

"I'm sweeping the storage room floor."

"Why?" he asks.

"Because you told me to find something to do."

"But the storage room floor doesn't need to be swept," he says. "Why don't you roll up that hose?"

I bite down on my lip. We're both grumpy, and I'm tired of working with Matt. Everything I do is wrong. We have been working in the garage for hours, and he only speaks to me when issuing an order. I hadn't seen this side of him when we were dating. With our busy work schedules, our time together was more limited, and we usually spent it eating at restaurants or at a friend's house; we didn't spend it working around his house. As I roll up the hose, it slides over my thighs and arms, getting snaky lines of mud all over me. "I'm taking a shower," I say. I know there has to be at least one spiderweb in my hair.

Matt works in the garage until he has rolled a second coat of paint on the floor and put away all of his supplies. He doesn't speak to me when he comes inside. He gets in the shower instead. As I sit in the living room, flipping through a novel, I feel lazy, guilty, tired, and confused. I am starting to realize how much spouses need to sacrifice to make a marriage work. And there is so much in Matt and me that has yet to surface. Before my wedding, my brother-in-law, Pat, said to me, "I never realized how much work went into a marriage, but that has in no way diminished my happiness in it." I hope Matt feels the same way. I'm starting to worry that he may regret having married me. Only time will reveal our true characters. And who knows what the future will bring?

TWELVE

The Ideology of an Unlocked Door: Making the World a Better Place

Marriage is one long conversation, checkered with disputes.

—Robert Louis Stevenson

*L*ater that night, Matt announced that he planned to leave the garage door open overnight while the EPOXYShield he had rolled over the concrete floor dried. According to the label on the back of the box, after four hours, you could walk on the painted floor, and, after seven days, you could drive on it without it peeling from the heat of your tires. I wasn't leaving the garage door up for seven days nor, for that matter, four hours. As a child, I saw my dad peel back our neighbor's porch screen to show her where a burglar had cut through it to climb into her house and steal her purse one night while she slept.

"If we shut the garage door, we'll get paint on the rubber seal on the bottom of it," Matt patiently explains. But that, I tell him, is a risk I am willing to take. "If you let a few criminals scare you, they win," he continues, because in Fargo a burglary merited the front page of the *Fargo Forum* and his family left the keys in the ignition of their parked cars. So it is on principle that he refuses to lock the doors at night and leaves the windows open when there is a warm breeze.

"But it's not safe," I say. We've argued about locking the doors before. If I leave for work first, I come home to a silent dark house with an unlocked front door. I stand in the foyer, imagining an intruder hiding in our bedroom closet behind the hanging jackets and pants and shirts. I listen for the creak of the closet door or footsteps shuffling across our carpet. If Matt takes off for work first, he leaves the garage door up while I'm standing beneath the shower spray, rinsing shampoo from my hair. "Do you know how many horror movies start that way?" I ask, as I tape a sign that reads "Please LOCK," the second word underlined, over the dead bolt on our front door.

I beg him to shut it, and, finally, he agrees. As I lie in bed, he goes downstairs to shut it, and its whirling motor comforts me. He returns to bed, and I snuggle up to him to feel his warmth, but I know this is not the end of our disagreement. Tomorrow, after he retrieves our newspaper from our porch steps, he will not turn to lock the door behind him. He will continue to his car.

When you're married, what do you do when your differences feel substantial? And how do you resolve a cyclical argument that you feel is threatening the stability of your marriage? What seems simple to me—locking the doors—has suddenly ballooned into a huge issue for us. And the next morning, I discover just how frustrating an impasse can be. When I go to the garage, I discover there is no paint on the seal, and I realize it's because Matt never shut the door.

"I did shut it," he says. "I left half of an inch between the seal and the floor."

"That's not shut," I say.

He laughs. "Jennifer, you're afraid of your own shadow," he says, because I compulsively lock our doors, even when we're both in the front yard pulling weeds. I know I'm a freak. I worry about everything. When I drive, I worry I'll hit a small child or a deer, and so I refuse to speed, even if I'm alone on an open highway in North Dakota. If I get stuck in traffic on my way to work, I worry I'll get fired upon arrival if I'm late. The unexpected ringing of our telephone after ten p.m. causes me to wonder if somebody has died.

"My sister was robbed at knifepoint in her apartment," I remind Matt. Although she wasn't harmed, she was tied up to her rocking chair while two masked men ransacked her apartment and took my grandmother's wedding ring from her finger.

"That was Washington, D.C.," he says, with his characteristic indifference to my irrelevant statistics. I tell him these things happen where we live, too. Minneapolis is not a small town. There are over one million people in our county, and Minneapolis has its share of crime. A few years ago, the *New York Times* dubbed it Murderapolis due to gang-related violence that claimed almost one hundred lives.

Brenda shares my need for security. Her husband, Mike, says she's turned their home into Fort Knox. But, like me, it drives her crazy to come home alone and find an unlocked door, an easy entry for an intruder. And Mike always forgets to lock the sliding glass door that leads to their screened-in porch.

I know I alarm easily. But Matt's apathy sits like hot ore inside of me, and like a woodpecker I start to drill into him. Over breakfast, I show him crime articles from our local newspaper and rattle off statistics I remember from sociology or read in women's magazines. He glances at the headlines and then smiles up at me.

"You and your facts," he says, amused. I have statistics on everything that could possibly harm us. That's a quirk I get from my dad, who constantly warns people about E. coli bacteria and the dangers of eating undercooked hamburgers.

Women see things differently, I tell him. On college campuses, we're taught about rape: You think that man's your friend? Wait until you're alone with him after he's been drinking. You pick up the paper and read what happened to that woman who went jogging alone, left a window open at night, or had one too many beers. And you feel for her, because you share her vulnerabilities. You wonder how she could have been so careless, until you find yourself walking down a dark street alone after bar closing, silently cursing your lack of judgment.

And that's why I want to shake Matt, because I feel he has put me on that dark street without realizing it. I want him to understand that the world isn't as safe as he perceives it to be, and, for most people, life isn't what it was for him in Fargo. I want him to be more like I am in this way; I want him to feel that injustice daily so that he will understand why we need to insulate ourselves against it.

But Matt can't do this. He only deals with injustice when he encounters it; he doesn't prepare for it in advance. When we were dating, I asked him how, as a trial lawyer, he knew whether somebody was lying to him. He looked puzzled. "I assume most people are telling the truth until they prove otherwise." How odd and how refreshing, I thought, that a partner at a national law firm assumes people don't lie.

"I assume people are lying until they prove otherwise," I responded, because I don't trust blindly as he does. It's easier and less risky to trust people less at the start, I think. But why am I afraid to be vulnerable? I'm starting to learn that our marriage will never succeed if I stay locked up inside myself, swallowed up by fear. I need to put myself out there.

But then time brought its own solution to our impasse. Early one morning, that crime I have been warning him about happens ten blocks from us. An eleven-year-old girl is attacked while sleeping in her bed. Her dad was gone for no more than a half hour while driving her mom to work. And the intruder entered through an unlocked door. Upon reading it, I'm like a hound after Matt when I find him eating breakfast in the kitchen. I make him read the article, too.

"Okay, I will start locking the doors," Matt says finally, after he finishes his bowl of raisin bran. He sets his bowl and spoon in the kitchen sink, and I return the milk and the orange juice to the refrigerator. With a napkin he wipes away the black smudge the newspaper has left on our kitchen table.

"Thank you," I say, but what I don't say is that I never want Matt to stop trusting, because it's through his eyes that I'm learning to see the good. But I do graciously accept his attempt to bend toward my point of view.

As always, he is true to his word. He starts locking the front door after he retrieves the Sunday newspaper from the front steps, the back door after he smokes the occasional cigar on the patio, the garage door after he retrieves the letters and catalogues and flyers from our mailbox. And so I remove the "Please LOCK" sign from the door, but have trouble getting the last bits of tape off.

THIRTEEN

The Morality of a Hard Day's Work

*Every man is his own ancestor, and every man
is his own heir. He devises his own future;
and he inherits his own past.*

—H. F. Hedge

For days, I stew over the bad feelings that linger from working in the garage with Matt. We can't do any joint projects without fighting. I don't understand his need to work. Have we gone from lovers to business partners or, worse yet, have we run out of things to say to one another? In marriage, patterns form quickly, and I'm not sure I like the one that is emerging: every Saturday morning, jolting ourselves from bed with an alarm clock that buzzes in the same way as a cock crows to tell the farmer that it is time to rise, working all day long beside Matt in silence.

Then we receive an unfortunate phone call. Matt's great uncle and namesake, Mathias Wetzstein, has died. We drive up to rural Carrington, North Dakota, to attend his funeral. I'm here to share in Matt's grief, in his family's grief, but I have no context for it. The farming life Uncle Math led is foreign to me. So, as

Matt drives, I stare out the car window at the endless prairie, but I can't tell where one property ends or another begins. "That's hay," Matt says, pointing at a field full of round hay bales, because it's so quiet that one of us has to say something. "And that stubble over there is the plowed-under remains of a wheat field." I nod, and we're quiet again.

We spend the night at the one hotel in Carrington, the Chieftain. The next morning, we drive to the church. At age eighty-four, Uncle Math becomes the first person the Carrington funeral director has ever buried in jeans. After the funeral, we drive to Uncle Math's farm to remove his belongings, some of which have been willed to Matt's dad, Clarence. This act seems cold to me; cleaning out his house seems too final, too sudden. But I'm quiet as we drive up the gravel road that ends before we arrive at the farm. We turn onto a long dirt road with electrical fencing running the length of it, and the farm, built into the gentle slope of the prairie, comes into view. I'm surprised to hear from Matt how few trees grow naturally on the flat land. Some were planted near the house to provide shelter from the harsh winter winds, but they look odd and out of place, too perfectly aligned. Weeds grow in the pastures, and the weathered wooden barns, which had once housed cattle, sheep, and hogs, hold rusting farm equipment.

Matt parks his truck in the grass and gets out to help his dad, Clarence, who, as a child, spent his summers working on this farm. His own father had died shortly after he turned five. Supporting five children proved too much of a hardship for his mother, and so every summer she sent Clarence to Uncle Math's, who quickly became a father figure for him. Clarence spent years following Uncle Math around the farm. I know Math's death is hard on him.

I watch Matt walk across the field, the high grass grazing his thighs. He looks strong and determined crossing the soft prairie. He disappears into one of the barns. I go inside, where his mom and sister are cleaning out the kitchen cabinets, packing dishes in cardboard boxes. The sod-and-stone house, each rock handpicked and laid by Uncle Math's parents, is built into a small hill, which allows it to be insulated by the earth. The ceilings in it feel unbearably low. I come close to knocking my forehead on a door frame. Matt's mom hands me a black garbage bag and points to the dresser I should start cleaning out. I feel bad digging into the drawers of a man I barely knew, deciding which of his life possessions are worth saving and which should be thrown away. I stand there for a moment before I begin watching Matt's aunt go around with her own box, putting dishes and record albums and crucifixes and photographs into it, things that other family members can use or may want. It's her way of continuing the circle of life.

Alongside Matt's mom and sister and aunt, I work more than I think I ever have in my life. After I finish cleaning out the dresser, stuffing jeans and button-down shirts into garbage bags, I wipe dust from the plastic horse figurines and family photographs on the shelves before boxing them up along with the plates. I scrub down the shelves and then sweep the wood floors. We all work in silence. The only time anybody speaks is to ask a question. I begin to feel lonely. Whenever I go outside to put one of the garbage bags into the trailer his dad has hauled up from Fargo, my eyes search the flat prairie for Matt. He's there, untangling a chain, or there, rolling a tire through the grass, or there, pulling wrenches and horse harnesses from the barn. He's too focused on his tasks to notice my halfhearted wave. For him, here and at home, work comes first, before us, I fear. I go back into the house, wiping the soot from my hands onto my jeans. I look around for more work to do, sticking my head into each room to see who needs help.

"This is how Clarence grieves," Matt's mom says to me quietly. "He throws himself into a project, and the project today is to clean the farm." Then I understand that this is how we will help Matt's dad grieve for Uncle Math. On a farm, there isn't always time to mourn. There's work to be done, which you must finish. You can't survive on the harsh prairie otherwise.

As the day progresses, I start to realize how much of your past influences who you are today, both as an individual and in your marriage. So much of who Matt is began here, on this farm, in the form of lessons that Uncle Math taught Clarence. "See work to do," the phrase which had so confused me when Matt uttered it, was what Uncle Math had repeatedly said to Clarence, because there was always work to be done on the farm: the lawn needed to be cut using scythes and grass hooks; the grass needed to be raked up and then put under trees to help the roots retain moisture; the rocks in the fields needed to be picked up so that they wouldn't damage the farm equipment. And that was the phrase Clarence repeated to his six children. "See work to do," he said, when they returned home from school. He didn't say it to teach his children how to work hard. He did it because there was work to be done. And many evenings they worked hard, dirty jobs, like scrubbing clean an oil tank they planned to use for a home-built sprinkler system, with Clarence working alongside them. Today, when Matt returns home from work, he notices what improvements we need to make to our home. That is how his eyes were trained.

And I finally understand why Matt finds so much satisfaction in spending a Saturday afternoon working. For Uncle Math, a lifelong bachelor, not to work was immoral. And so he found satisfaction in each of his accomplishments, like filling his haymow with freshly cut hay or his grain bin with harvested grain.

Even in the winter, when the temperature plummeted to thirty below zero and the wind whipped the snow into such frenzy that even the sky looked white, he still took food and water to his horses. Through him, Clarence learned that not to work was immoral. Once, Clarence told me that even today he doesn't sleep well at night. When he closes his eyes, he thinks about what he can build or modify. Recently, while his wife was out of town, he flipped on the television during the afternoon and saw there was a movie on. Although he felt guilty for not working, he said, "I am sixty-two years old. For the first time in my life, I will sit here and watch a movie." And he did. When it was over, fearing he had wasted an afternoon, he walked outside to see how his horses were doing. And he shared that lesson with Matt. For a day to not feel like a waste, Matt, like his dad, needs to see at least one tangible achievement, even if it is nothing more than a well-swept garage. While in theory he knows that quality time together improves our marriage, he finds it difficult to quantify that. And so, for him, tasks for which he can see an end result take precedence over our leisure time together. He'd rather expend our time and energy on projects around the house, work for which he can see an immediate end result. Work comes first, as it did for Uncle Math and Clarence.

And I'm beginning to understand why Matt feels no pity for me when I show him my hands blistered from raking. Uncle Math, with no experience with children, treated young Clarence as an adult and gave him a job. At age six, Clarence started driving the tractor, pulling a rake, which swept up the hay behind him. He got his first sick day at seven when he jammed a rusty pitchfork into his foot while trying to spear a bundle of barley. He had wanted to set the bundle upright so that it wouldn't rot from lying on the ground in water, should it rain. But the pitchfork had gone straight through the bundle and into the arch of his foot. The pain shot straight up his back to his eyes. Since it had missed all major vessels, nobody called a doctor. His aunt simply yanked it out. Uncle Math bandaged it, and gave him a half day off. And Clarence passed this lesson on to Matt. One summer, as Matt stood on a ladder staining the house, his arms, splattered with stain, began to burn in the hot sun. But Matt knew that if he didn't finish the job, somebody else would have to complete it. Many times he had witnessed his dad finish a job despite terrible weather, a finger smashed with a hammer, or a bad back. He knew that for Clarence, and therefore for him, leaving a job incomplete was not an option. And that is why, for Matt, my blisters are not an obstacle that should prevent me from finishing any job to which I've been assigned.

With this knowledge I will be more tolerant of Matt's behavior. He sees his ability to work hard, which his dad has given him, as a gift, and he's right. It has benefited him professionally. Through his hard work he obtained a law degree with honors and became a partner in his firm. But I wish there was a way I could convince him to apply his work ethic to our marriage as well, to see the work that it requires. Matt doesn't seem to think a marriage should necessitate any work.

Honestly, with as much as we've been fighting lately, I'm starting to wonder if we'll make it. It's not that I want us to constantly sacrifice for one another, giving up important parts of ourselves. What I want is a marriage that takes from each of us the best we have to offer. In marriage, you have to commit to your new family. Whatever your family legacy may be, you can't let it dictate your future. You have the power to make your own decisions, to take control of your life so that you don't repeat the past. As different people with different needs, Matt and I require our own marital blueprint from which to work, not one that has been handed down from one generation to the next.

Early Sunday morning, Matt and I drive back to Minneapolis with Uncle Math's dusty phonograph in the backseat. It's a beautiful antique piece with a slightly musty smell. We plan to show it in our living room as a concrete reminder of a part of the past that has been lost. Thinking about where exactly to put it makes me wonder if any bride realizes how much family will influence her marriage before she marries. I know I didn't.

When we return to Minneapolis, Matt wants to unload the truck, remove the McDonald's hamburger wrappers and paper cups from beneath the seats, put our dirty clothes into the washing machine, and set our empty suitcases in the storage room— all before we get the mail, listen to our phone messages, or check e-mail. In the past, I would have dismissed him, said I'd finish those tasks later. But now that I understand the principle behind why he feels we must do our chores first, I help him without complaining, finally seeing some of the work that needs to be done.

FOURTEEN

The Starter Marriage

The worst reconciliation is better than the best divorce.
–Cervantes

ere we are, sitting in front of our fireplace, muddling through yet another issue that has arisen so early on in our marriage. There's no heat between us, no intensity in our debate, just words carelessly tossed out, hoping they land and stick where they should, accusations we've both heard before, for which we have packaged, emotionless responses. Only this argument ends differently. Matt, looking beyond me, asks, "Do you want to be married?" Although he looks at the painting hanging on the wall behind me, his countenance reveals that he's worried my answer will hurt. Immediately, I am overcome with guilt. I respond with, "Of course," but I'm not sure I mean it. And I know my answer is not convincing.

While he's the first one of us to ask this question, he may not be the first to think about the answer to it. Now that our honeymoon period is over and we have to navigate complicated marital issues, I've wondered on more than one occasion if we'll make it. We seem to be at that crossroad of *should we stay together or divorce?* much earlier than I expected. Will we simply become what Pamela Paul defines as a starter marriage in her book, *The Starter Marriage and the Future of Matrimony*? Matt and I fit her profile: both of us are under thirty-five and have no children. And we're both concerned that our marriage won't last. I know that you can find happiness a second time around, as some of my divorced twenty-something friends have. And much of the social stigma surrounding divorce is gone. So, I wonder, do first marriages act as starter marriages, a sort of trial marriage, one in which you figure out who you are and what you want so that the next time around you can marry for a lifetime? And, if so, will I be dissolving mine soon? To be honest, I hate that constant feeling of vulnerability in marriage, that all your happiness can go away with one snap of his fingers; that there is no control, just trust. With marriage, there is another person involved, and you can't control them or their actions. No matter how hard you try, sometimes you just can't make your relationship work. So is divorce an easy way out? And, if so, how do you know when enough is enough?

I look to my friend, Emily, for an answer. She had a starter marriage. She's smart and intelligent, flexible and kind, with all sorts of interests. I've always secretly wondered how a marriage of hers could fail. Divorce, it seems, often occurs when two perfectly normal people just can't make it work. So what happened? Was her ex-husband just too different from her? Or did they simply lose the energy to hold on to each other? I hope that by understanding why her marriage failed, I can somehow save my own, or at least predict what our future holds. And so, one day, as we're jogging together, I gently broach the subject with her. I try not to sound accusatory about her divorce. Who knows where

Matt and I will be in life and in marriage down the road? But, to my surprise, she is very open with me.

She says she met her ex-husband, Mark, during their first week of law school and was immediately attracted to him. He was adorable and self-confident, friendly and unpretentious, and incredibly open. From the start, she had that gut instinct that Mark got her, and she got him. Unlike past boyfriends, he supported and understood any difficulties she encountered with her family. And he could discuss politics and foreign policy as passionately as she could.

"Did you ever see any red flags while you were dating?" I ask her, because her ex, whom I've never met, sounds perfect for her. I know that everybody has their faults and in all relationships red flags exist. I saw red flags when it came to Matt, and I know that he saw some when it came to me. So how do you know which ones you should pay attention to, and which ones you should overlook?

"Our biggest red flag was that we could never resolve conflict," she says, and that concerns me. Matt and I don't seem equipped to resolve conflict either. Our arguments don't have endings, they continuously loop. But then she goes on. "Once, when we were jogging, we got into a silly fight. He turned around and ran in the opposite direction, leaving me standing there alone on the sidewalk. And he could be manipulative. When we were dating, he'd threaten to break up with me. When we were engaged, he'd threaten to call off the wedding. But we had so much fun together—I loved him so much—that I decided to overlook much of his behavior while we were dating."

"When did you know you were getting divorced?" I ask.

"It was shortly after our one-year anniversary," she says. They had arranged to stay at a hotel to celebrate. Over dinner, they got into an argument. She doesn't remember over what. After they finished eating, they went back to their room to dress for the hot tub. When she put on her bathing suit, he called her a fat pig. "He was emotionally abusive," she says. "For him to feel like I loved him, he had to get a big emotional reaction from me. He didn't believe me when I simply said it. By making me cry, he knew I cared. So, whenever we argued, he tried all sorts of ways to get back at me. He'd tell me I wasn't a good cook, and I'd laugh. He'd tell me I had no friends, and I'd laugh. He'd tell me I wasn't good at school, and I'd laugh. And he'd keep going until he found my sensitive spot and then zoned in on it—like my weight. And then he'd feel better about himself as I cried."

Emily knew she couldn't continue on in her relationship as it was. And so, shortly after that night, they agreed to separate. One morning, she handed Mark the classified section from the newspaper in which she had circled apartments for him. That night, after work, she returned home to find that he had packed up and left. She collapsed on the couch and sobbed. There was no one there to lift her spirits up, no warm body to cling to at night. It was the worst day of her life, she says. It was when the reality of it all sank in. They had spent only one night apart since they married, and here she was indefinitely alone in their apartment. She still felt that emotional bond that linked her to Mark, as unhealthy as it was.

She tried to repair their marriage. She asked Mark to attend therapy with her, and he committed to ten sessions, after which he'd make a decision about their marriage. To each session he'd bring a list of Emily's faults for the psychologist to review. But the psychologist wouldn't side with him. So, after nine sessions, he quit going. Still, Emily was hopeful. She attended the last session alone. But then the psychologist said that for all of the times she had heard Emily say she wanted to make her marriage work, she had never once heard Mark say that. And that, Emily says, was when she realized her marriage would never work.

To myself, I think, "Good riddance. That must have been a liberating moment for her." But her divorce didn't deliver her the happiness I expected it would. Instead, it was incredibly painful for her. The future she had been planning for—a new home, children, in-laws—was inextricably linked to her and Mark's togetherness. What would her future bring her now? It loomed before her, a dark chasm. What she quickly discovered was that divorce was harder than she expected. Emily, always a success, had publicly failed at her biggest undertaking in her personal life.

It took her a year to start dating again. And that first year of dating was difficult for her. She had no confidence in her ability to judge what made for a good relationship and what didn't. But now, years later, she is happy in a committed relationship with a man who has never once been unkind to her. "All relationships will have good times and bad times," she says. "But what you have to look at are the bad times. How does your partner treat you then? Is there physical or emotional abuse?" This is the first response of hers that I find comforting. Matt is always fair and respectful when we argue.

For me, Emily's story is like one of those near-death experiences you read about, where your life flashes before your eyes. The fallout of a divorce can be greater than or equal to your pain in your marriage. I realize that the pain of learning to live with Matt would never compare to the pain of losing him. Finally I'm seeing how much good there is in our marriage worth preserving. And, when I ask myself, do you think you could find a better partner than Matt, or do you simply want a partner who handles your weaknesses better, I'm ashamed of what my answer is.

I am not Emily, and Matt is not Mark. While their ending makes me fearful, I refuse to let that fear derail our marriage. And so I return home to Matt willing to do whatever it takes to restore our marriage. "Of course I want to be married to you," I say, and I mean it wholeheartedly.

FIFTEEN

You're in My Space

*Learn the wisdom of compromise, for it is better to
bend a little than to break.*

—Jane Wells

I adore Matt, but I'm starting to feel a little cramped living
with him. Because while I may not be neat, his stuff is like
algae: it grows and spills into each room. He has plaid shirts in
the guest bedroom closet, ski clothes in the office closet, and
jackets with varsity lettering from his high school days in the
main closet. But my biggest pet peeve is his reading material—
newspapers, magazines, and books—that covers most surfaces in
our home. On his bedside table is a *New Yorker* issue from
1997, which he refuses to throw out because there's an article in
it that he wants to read.

"Don't you think that if you haven't read it by now, there's a
good chance you never will?" I ask. He shrugs.

I ask Christina and my friend Anne, who recently married,
how they are adjusting to living with their spouses. Christina says
that Rob has been respectful of her desire not to let clutter build
on their dining room table. He's given up his habit of emptying

his pocket contents there. But what they're struggling with is their differing tastes in artwork. Rob's friend is a painter, and sometimes his themes tend to be dark and disturbing. While Christina loves his brushstrokes and his style, she doesn't want an oil painting of a dead naked woman hanging over her dining room table. "What does that say about us that we have chosen this depressing piece of artwork?" she says, and I laugh when I think about Christina entertaining dinner guests beneath it. She asked Rob to hang the painting in the basement, and he did. But, as a compromise, they went over to his friend's apartment and bought one they both liked.

And Anne has come up with a solution to finding her husband Pete's pocket contents all over her house. "You never know what will come out of his pockets—screws, nuts, bolts," she jokes. As he doesn't have a day planner, he'd write reminders for himself on yellow Post-it notes, which she'd find on their coffee table, end tables, kitchen counter, and dining room table. She used to ask him to pick up after himself, but found he'd simply move his stuff in piles from the living room to the office, from the office to the bedroom. "You'd think he were a guest in our home," she says, because he rarely puts his belongings in his drawers and she constantly has to help him find what he has lost. And so now she puts whatever she finds lying around the house—business cards, paper clips, receipts, and those yellow Post-it notes—on his nightstand. Her plan is to buy a plastic bin for him from Target, which she'll store under their bed, if he doesn't clean off his nightstand soon.

All of us find that living together is an adjustment. So I try to remind myself that for all the compromises I have to make to live with Matt, he is making just as many compromises to live with me, like readjusting his no-more-than-two-towels-in-the-bathroom rule, which I constantly break because I need an additional one with which to wrap my wet hair. But what's hard is just when we think we've reached a compromise, we find we must compromise on our compromise.

Take for instance Matt's change cup. Tired of picking up the pennies that overflow from it, I bought him an electronic change sorter to replace it. He humored me by playing with his new sorter for a few days. He dumped his coins into it and then watched his pennies, nickels, dimes, and quarters sort, each dropping into its own slot. But a week later, he took all of the change out of the sorter and put it back into his change cup.

"What are you doing?" I asked him, astonished.

"I take money out of the change cup before I leave for work for my morning cup of coffee," he said. "That's what I do."

"Why can't you take money out of the sorter? That way your coins won't spill onto the dresser." I know he'll never get around to spending all of those pennies. At least if they're wrapped I can exchange them at the bank for dollar bills.

"Because that's not how I do it," he said. "And besides, the sorter is four times the size of the change cup. To get money out of it, you have to open it up, unwrap the change, put the wrappers back into their slots, and then close it." I argued; I cajoled. It was no use; he wanted his change cup. He intoned every cliché he could think of, enjoying his rhymes: "A change cup filled with change is as American as apple pie and the Fourth of July." I feared he'd break out into song and dance. To me, a change cup was nothing more than an old, chipped coffee cup that shouldn't have been salvaged, but what can you do. I guess it's true; you never really know somebody until you live with him. And it wasn't until after we married that I discovered how important Matt's physical habits are to him.

But I'm trying to be flexible for him, because I know how

much the disorder I create frustrates him. I don't notice the mud that my shoes streak across the kitchen floor or my socks crumpled on the bathroom floor. Nor do I see the ponytail holder I've left on the coffee table or the hairbrush I've set down beside the kitchen sink. Occasionally he finds one of my out-of-place belongings and asks, "Is this yours?" What he's really asking is for me to put it away, but I answer with a simple, "Yes," because I want him to ask his questions directly.

"Where does it go?"

"Why don't you put it next to your newspapers?" I say. "Maybe then you'll remember to pick them up."

He's quiet for a moment. "Your shoes are all over the place," he says, and I look into the foyer at the pair I kicked off. One lies on its side against the wall. I see four pairs of Matt's shoes, all perfectly lined up with his sneaker laces tucked in.

"Your shoes make more of a mess because there are more of them," I say.

"But my shoes are straight," he says.

This is bad. We've started responding to criticism with criticism, the most unproductive way to solve our problem. We need to work together to decide what is fair. In marriage, there are no limits to what has to be negotiated. So we stop saying "You always" and "You never" and talk about what we expect from each other. We don't interrupt each other or defend ourselves; we simply listen to our spouse's feelings. And then we compromise on a rule that suits us both: "Out of sight, out of mind." We agree that everything has a place, where it must go at the end of each day. And if something is not picked up, we gently remind the other to put it away.

SIXTEEN

What Is a Lie?

One falsehood spoils a thousand truths.
—Saying (Ashanti)

While driving Matt's truck down the road—my car is in the shop—I start craving Taco Bell's hard-shell tacos loaded with meat and cheese and salsa. Matt, I know, keeps money in his center console, so I open it and dig through it, pulling out some dollar bills. I find enough cash for two hard-shell tacos and a diet Coke. And I find a rectangular pink slip. Out of curiosity, I unravel it. It is a receipt for a pistol, dated six months before our wedding. I stare down at it, so angry that at first I don't respond when the crackly voice comes through the Taco Bell intercom asking for my order. Stupidly, I check behind my seat for the gun. Nothing there except a sweatshirt. What about the glove compartment? Nope, just maps, receipts, and his truck manual. So where is it?

While we were dating, Matt mentioned that he planned to buy a pistol eventually to use at the shooting range. Like many people I have met in the Midwest, Matt feels very comfortable around guns. He grew up with them in the house, and his dad taught him to shoot one when he was eight years old. His brothers Luke and Walter embark on an annual deer hunting trip, and use the meat to prepare delicious spicy sausages, jerky, and venison steaks for their family, which, I have to admit, I've thoroughly enjoyed. When Matt's dad rides his horses in the Rocky Mountains, he always carries a pistol in case of bears. Matt feels shooting as a sport is a natural continuation of his upbringing.

While I can appreciate his point of view, I think having a gun in the house makes it more likely your children will accidentally shoot themselves or you. Matt thinks you should keep your gun locked in a safe in your house but that you should teach your kids how to use it. Hunting, he says, helps children learn about the frailty of life and earn respect for nature. And he believes that gun ownership comes with responsibility. He doesn't support the right to carry semiautomatic assault weapons and is not opposed to reasonable gun regulations.

While we were dating, I had tried to argue him out of his purchase, and thought I had succeeded. I made it clear that I don't like guns of any sort—shotguns, pistols, or rifles. To me they symbolize a need for power, for control, an ornament of masculinity, or self-protection gone awry. And Matt, who can keep control of any situation with his quick wit, doesn't need a pistol.

When I discover Matt owns a pistol, I feel betrayed. I wonder what else I don't know about him. Has he kept other things hidden from me? In a relationship, learning to trust one another can be challenging, taking years sometimes. But, as difficult as trust can be to establish, destroying it is much quicker—in one moment.

I confront Matt as soon as he walks through the front door, before he has time to take off his suit jacket or put down his leather briefcase. "I found your receipt for your pistol," I say, and he doesn't respond at first. He looks at the pink receipt I'm clutching in my hand and smiles gently, a loving smile. I don't smile back.

"Dear, I got it before we were married," he says. "I wanted to tell you about it, but I wasn't sure how you'd react." He puts down his briefcase and sits next to me on the couch. Matt, I have learned, definitely sees a difference in the loyalty you have to a girlfriend than what you have to a wife. And for this reason I can excuse some of his past errors in judgment—like purchasing this pistol without telling me—because for him we were still two separate entities. But what I don't like is that he didn't tell me that he owned one after we were married.

"Where is it?"

"It's at Parker's house. You have always said that you do not want a gun in our house. I respected your wishes. I never brought the pistol home," he says. He remains calm, too calm, and that frustrates and confuses me. I stare at him, trying to decide whether I should forgive him since he didn't bring the pistol in the house, or be angrier because he's shared his secret of having it with a mutual friend. He takes advantage of my confusion.

"You can't be upset," he continues. "That was an illegal search and seizure. Any evidence you obtained is excluded per the Fourth Amendment."

"You lied to me," I say.

"That's not a lie," Matt says. "You never said that I couldn't buy a gun. You just said that I couldn't bring it into the house." Matt believes you must be completely honest at all times. If he answers a phone call for me that I do not wish to take, he will not tell the person that I am not home.

"An omission is a lie because you intended to deceive me," I argue. "And a lie erodes trust. Without trust, we cannot have a relationship. You cannot lie to me again."

But Matt, who is a master at structuring a phrase just so, like a magician creating an illusion with lights and costumes, is not convinced he lied. "You said you didn't want a gun in the house. I honored your request." He tries to pick up my hand, but I pull away. I can't think when he's touching me.

"Matt, I can't trust you if you're going to take advantage of every little loophole you find in my arguments," I say. Omitting those loopholes would require I plan every conversation in advance. He thinks for a moment, and then says that for the sake of our relationship, he'll ask for clarification when he's unsure of what my position is.

My friend Anne, whose husband, Pete, is an attorney, describes this phenomenon as *lawyerese*. *Lawyerese*, she says, is different from *legalese*, which is a convoluted language in which lawyers use every obscure word they know and then sum up their point with a Latin phrase. *Lawyerese* is like a tap dance, where so much noise is created and the movements are so fast that you can't quite grasp the individual steps. In their routine, they dance through the loopholes in your argument to give you a truth, just not the one you expected. It's not until the final curtain falls that you realize you've lost this argument on a series of technicalities for which you didn't plan.

But a month later, I find myself more sympathetic with Matt's position when he asks me to put a house key under our front doormat for his mom who is arriving that weekend. "Okay," I say, although for safety reasons I have no intention of leaving it there for three days. But if I say that I'll do it on the morning of her arrival, we'll argue about it. He'll want to do it now so that we won't forget. So on this occasion I decide to take the, "What he doesn't know won't hurt him" approach, as it's easier than arguing. You do what you can to avoid an argument. But then

Mr. Responsible does something irresponsible: while we are at the lake, he locks his keys in his truck. Through the window we see them lying on the driver's seat sparkling in the sun.

"Good thing you put that key out," he says, and I have to tell him I didn't. He doesn't react at first. He stands there with his mouth slightly open, thinking about what to say.

"What happened to 'an omission is a lie'?" he said.

"I intended to put the key out before your mom arrived."

"But you told me you would do it on Wednesday."

I defend myself. "Putting the key under the doormat is a security risk," I say. "I would have put the key out by the time she arrived. I had a definite ending date for following through." But the truth is that I perceive my omission differently because it's mine. It won't erode the trust I have for myself. I realize my lie was self-serving, with the intent to deceive him, so I stop talking. I need to think.

So what is a lie? Merriam-Webster defines a lie as, "to make an untrue statement with intent to deceive," or "to create a false or misleading impression." It's difficult to be open and truthful with your spouse, but you need to be strong enough within yourself to do so. Because no matter what form your lie takes—an omission, a secret, or a deliberate misstatement—you'll erode trust. And, without trust, what kind of marriage will you have?

"I'm sorry," I say to Matt. It's never too late to try to regain your spouse's trust. "I shouldn't have lied." I swear to myself that from now on I'll try to be honest, as difficult as the battles ahead may be.

SEVENTEEN

Petty Fights

The art of being wise is the art of knowing what to overlook.
—William James

During times of stress, Matt and I can bicker over a million things in the course of one day. Every little thing we do affects the other. And Matt, as a perfectionist, usually has an opinion about a number of issues, like how close to the garage wall I should park my car, at what speed I should drive on highways, and how I should fold our T-shirts. I generally don't have an opinion, at least not a strong one. And often I don't have patience for him, either. Matt says that I have a two-hour limit with him before I start to get annoyed. And he's right. I feel my skin start to prickle. I snap. "Do you really need to have control over every little insignificant issue in our lives?" I ask. But, for him, there is a right way—his way—and a wrong way—usually my way—to do something.

But our most petty, repetitive fight, which neither of us can let go of, is over the temperature of the thermostat. "We need to keep it set at sixty-eight degrees," he says, and checks to make sure I haven't rolled the dial any higher. "Setting it any higher wastes money and energy." Lately, Matt has become quite the environmentalist. But, as I sit there with a turtleneck and a sweatshirt on, a blanket wrapped around my legs, I think about what a hypocrite he is. In the summer, when Mother Nature turns up the heat, he has no problem running the air conditioner so high that I need to wear a sweater then, too. I'm always cold in our house.

There are three things that immediately put me in a bad mood: being tired, being hungry, or being cold. And, when I'm with Matt, I'm usually cold. During winter, when we drive to Fargo, he sets the truck's heat so low that I ride with my coat on and his draping my lap. I can't get Matt to understand how much my bones hurt as he's sitting there sweating in his T-shirt. "It's all a matter of willpower," he says. That's one thing about Matt: he's not the greatest empathizer if he can't see your point. And it's frustrating that in marriage I just can't turn up the heat when I'm cold. While most of the time marriage makes my life easier and better, sometimes—like now—it makes it ridiculously hard and tiring, as you negotiate every little boundary.

How do most newlyweds decide which battles to fight? Everybody has basic values and principles they need to defend. But what about all of those relatively unimportant stances you've taken throughout your life? How do you reconcile those with your husband's?

Christina has found a way to resolve one of her petty fights with Rob. As a lawyer that works with a food company, she's a food safety nut. And Rob thinks nothing of lifting cooked chicken and steaks from the grill using the same utensils that touched the raw meat. "You have to wash those first," she hollered, the first time she saw him do it. To appease her, he took the tongs inside and ran them under hot water, but she knew that wouldn't kill bacteria like E. coli. For a while, they constantly argued over what constituted proper food safety, but soon Christina decided that this wasn't an issue worth fighting over. Rather, she carefully watches Rob through the kitchen window as he grills. When a piece of raw meat leaves a plate, she rushes out with a clean one and snatches the tainted one. And, whenever he puts the tongs down, she washes them.

Brenda, meanwhile, is trying to let go of the petty things that bother her, like Mike's mail, which he leaves on the kitchen counter for weeks, sometimes months, even. She'll ask him to pick it up and then come home to find it still sitting there. Like Matt and Christina, she likes order in her home, and, when she doesn't get it, her face will show her irritation. "What's wrong?" Mike will ask her, but she doesn't want to explain to him how all she can think about right now is why he didn't remove his pile of mail from their counter, as she's asked. As she doesn't want to continuously pester him, she'll respond with, "Nothing," as she tries to let go of it, to stop allowing little things like his cardboard boxes in their storage room, which she thinks will rot if he doesn't unpack them soon, from bothering her. But her answer will make Mike worry that he's committed a serious error, and he will push an answer out of her. And then when she confesses that that's it—it's just the mail on the counter or his boxes in their storage room—he'll look at her, both confused and relieved, and say, "That's it?" And sometimes his laugh will break the tension between them.

But Matt and I are still struggling to define our boundaries. One Saturday afternoon, after he leaves for work, I turn the thermostat up to seventy-four. I'm finally warm enough to remove the blanket from my lap. I no longer feel a chill along the back of my neck. For once I am comfortable in my own home.

But then I don't remember to turn the thermostat down before he returns home from work. This is my passive-aggressive nature. I'll pretend that I'm okay with what Matt has said and then I'll do what he asked me not to behind his back. And he is not happy with me when he returns home.

"If you turn the thermostat past seventy-two, you run the risk of damaging the furnace," he says. I look at him suspiciously. Although neither of us is overly mechanical, Matt, having studied to be an engineer, is able to offer technical arguments that I'm ill-equipped to rebut.

"But I'm cold!" I say.

"Then why don't you put on another sweater?" he asks. But I already have on a sweater and socks and sweatpants. I don't need more layers; I need heat.

That night, as we dress for bed, I put on a pair of Matt's old thick, cotton sweatpants, a sweatshirt, and wool socks. I'm done fighting for my share of the comforter in a room as chilled as a refrigerator.

"You have on more clothes than an Eskimo," Matt says.

"I'll put on my pajamas if you turn up the heat," I say. "Otherwise, I'll freeze all night long." He doesn't take the bait. So we climb into bed together, and we're both annoyed. Only his breathing quickly deepens and slows, while I lie awake staring up at the ceiling. I've realized that that adage, "Never go to bed angry," applies only to women, because men just fall asleep. I can't sleep next to him when I'm upset, and, as I listen to him breathe, wonder how he can rest so easily when he should be feeling guilty. Finally, I get out of bed and lie down on the couch, completely annoyed that he's not out here when he's the one who is wrong.

Matt doesn't want me sleeping on the couch again. And so the next night, he gives in and agrees to raise the thermostat by two degrees. I feel like an equal in our partnership. I switch back to my own pajamas, but I keep my socks on. Matt finds this look—me in a nightgown with bobby socks on—completely unromantic.

"Take your socks off," he says.

"Turn the heat up higher," I retort. "I'll take off one sock per degree."

He watches me like prey from his side of the bed. I stand there amused, ready to dodge whatever move he makes. Suddenly, he lunges and grabs one of my arms and pulls me onto the bed. He tries to rip my socks off, but I flail my legs and kick him off. I slip out of his hold. But he's stronger than I am, and once again he's got me pinned. This time he manages to yank off one of my socks.

We look at each other and laugh and laugh and laugh. We're so completely ridiculous right now. We're discovering the millions of little differences between us as we try hard to draw our marital boundaries. There's nothing too stupid over which to argue. It's funny that I can't sleep without my socks on, and it's even funnier that it bothers him. Humor, we're discovering, is a great tool for working through our issues. Because the thing is, you won't remember the million things you bickered over—like who should take out the trash, do the dishes, or make the bed. But what you will remember, as will your spouse, is how you felt during your disagreements. Every day you make choices as to how to show—or not show—your love for the person you're married to, and those choices affect your future. Pick your battles; it's no fun living in a constant state of tension. We stop wrestling and just lie in each other's arms. Marriage is fun, I realize.

We still occasionally argue over the thermostat, but we've let go of many of our petty fights. It's easier to negotiate what you need and want in a loving environment, rather than a hostile one. Matt's learning to be more flexible, and to let go of having control over insignificant issues. And, as I become accustomed to his personality, I have more patience with him. Sometimes things have a way of working out in the end.

EIGHTEEN

CEO versus COO

Light is the task when many share the toil.
–Homer

One morning, over breakfast, Matt announces that he has come up with an analogy for our marriage. "It's like I'm the CEO and you're the COO. I'm responsible for our long-term strategy, while you're responsible for the day-to-day operations." Is he serious? I just stare at him, unable to respond.

"Specialization of labor is what makes the work force efficient," Matt argues. Does it make sense to have a division of labor at home? It's true that he's often the visionary in our household. It was his idea to replace the carpet and build a new retaining wall and pull trees from around the perimeter of our house before their roots cracked our foundation. But what I've discovered is that while Matt is the master of ideas, he is not always the master implementer. Like a CEO, he wakes each morning with ten great ideas that he assigns to me, with no clue as to how much work goes into getting the job done. He spends more time preparing his honey to-do list than I spend planning dinner.

The list was my idea. While some newlyweds may react to a to-do list, I encourage it. Domestic disorder doesn't bother me. I don't notice what needs to be done around the house, and so Matt feels as if all household maintenance, like changing lightbulbs, calling the plumber for a leaky faucet, or repairing a loose doorknob falls to him. While he tackles these household tasks with zest, I'm starting to realize that he needs his downtime, too. And, with my relaxed attitude, he isn't getting it. So we use our task list to negotiate. Through it, I know what Matt expects of me, and he feels like I'm supporting him by contributing equally to the upkeep of our household. And having a task list makes managing a household feel less overwhelming to me. As somebody who's heard, "You'd forget your head if it weren't attached to your body," for her entire life, I could never remember half the things Matt asked me to do before walking out the door. And we've agreed that if the task isn't written down, Matt can't complain if I forget to do it. But still, I'm not sure that I want the role of a COO in marriage. I don't spend my days at a call center designed for wives; I have a career to which I need to attend, too.

How do most spouses divide up the housework? Anne, as the CEO in her household, thrives on having a master task list, and always has. She has been organizing since birth. As a child, she'd make lists for herself with every little task she could think of, like brush your teeth, get dressed, and make your bed, just to feel that thrill of crossing an item off. She has continued making lists in marriage. Recently, she left her handwritten one for Pete—and he lost it. Now she's driving herself crazy trying to remember what she had written on it. "I could deal with him not finishing the tasks on it, but losing it?" she says. "Now even I don't know what needs to be done!" She's plagued by her worries that none of those tasks will get done. And so she's frantically putting together an Excel spreadsheet, into which she can enter and prioritize their tasks, and for which she'll have a back-up copy. While Pete does not share Anne's thrill in crossing out a completed task, he is starting to appreciate that she emotionally interprets what he does or does not do in terms of her list. And so he is trying to support her needs by finishing his assigned tasks.

On a Saturday afternoon, Matt announces another brilliant idea. "We need to get our life organized," he says, "We should make a filing system." "We" refers to who gets the credit, not who does the work. So I refuse to write "filing system" on my list until he specifically asks me to design it. "When do you think you'll have it finished?"

"I'm not sure," I say. "I should get to it in a day or two." I should know not to give him a vague deadline. When it comes to his task list, he has a weird sense of urgency. I used to e-mail him after I'd completed one of his tasks, but he'd respond to my lengthy e-mails with a one-word response like, "Great" or "Okay." Insulted, I stopped e-mailing him. Now, as soon as he returns home, he pesters me about whatever tasks are on the list—even irrelevant ones like refilling the soap dispenser in the guest bathroom—until I get them done.

And later that week, I finally burst like a water pipe. "Stop!" I yell, flooded with frustration. "Don't ask me one more question about the list! I don't want to talk to you about the list until Saturday. That is the only day you can ask for a status update, and that is the only day you can assign me tasks." We all have our own internal body clocks, our own sense of timing. Nagging only creates tension. I will start on the filing system when I feel ready to do it.

And, later that evening, I begin working on it. I actually do some online research to determine how best to categorize the cabinet, knowing how picky Matt is. I print labels for the manila folders and hanging folders; I design an outline of the file layout as a guide and tape it to the side of the cabinet; I tuck all of the papers that were previously piled on the office desk into the manila sleeves and integrate some of Matt's old files into our new system.

That Saturday, I allow Matt to inspect our new filing system. He's thrilled. He loves efficiency and organization and clean lines in his office—a bare desk, an empty in-box, a clear hutch, all of which a filing system provides. And he's great at showing his gratitude. I flush with pride at his praise. But, a few nights later, when he can't find his tax returns, I realize I've made a grave mistake. Like Anne and her Tupperware drawer, I am now permanently tied to the filing system, as I am the only one who knows how to use it.

"Taxes start with the letter T," I say, in my attempt to train him. "Think alphabetically."

"Let me tell you how Barb organizes our files at work," he says, and I stop him right there. Barb is his assistant at work who he thinks is perfect.

"Silence is consent," I tell him. "If you do not help me in the planning stages, then you can't criticize the end result. If you want the filing cabinet to be organized differently, then you need to redo it." I firmly believe that you have to allow your spouse to complete a task in his or her own way.

I don't think housework can ever be even or fairly divided. But you do need to work with your spouse to come up with some guidelines that work for you. Matt's learning to pick and choose which projects are important to him, and to give me credit when

I complete my tasks. And I am learning how to follow through on my promise to do an equal share of the work by doing a little each day. Both of us are discovering that domestic chores are becoming less draining emotionally and physically, as well as less taxing on our marriage.

NINETEEN

I Have a Life

I cannot love you and be perfectly satisfied at such a distance from you.
—Elizabeth Sheridan

My phone rings at work and I answer it with my most professional voice. "Hello, dear," I hear, and instantly I recognize Matt's warm voice. I press the phone tighter against my ear. He informs me that his business trip to Dallas has been canceled. "I thought after work we could meet at the gym and then have sushi together." I smile. This is probably my favorite date with him. He lifts weights while I alternate between admiring his reflection in the mirror and flipping through a women's magazine while climbing a StairMaster. Afterwards we shower in the locker rooms—I love to indulge in all of the free hygiene products, like the deodorant, razors, hair spray, Q-Tips, and mouthwash—before meeting at the third-floor restaurant.

But tonight I have soccer. And teams don't take kindly to you not showing up at the last minute. If they're forced to play a player down, they'll likely lose. While some players take it more seriously than others, everybody on the team likes to win. I, too, have a competitive spirit. In all honesty, I'd rather have dinner with Matt than play soccer. But I believe that when you have plans with people depending on you, you don't cancel them because something better comes along.

"I have soccer tonight," I say.

"Can't you skip it?" he asks. This is a sore spot for us. I'd rather have an overbooked schedule than an underbooked one, and so here's what's on my social calendar for this week: soccer on Monday and Saturday, girls' night on Wednesday, and touch football on Thursday. Mix that in with Matt's schedule of travel, business dinners, friends, family, and recreational basketball, and you can see why we're struggling to find time for each other. I know that sometimes it's hard for him to control his schedule. He has little free time. When space opens up, he'd like to spend time with me. But if I don't fill my calendar and plan ahead, then half the time I sit home alone at night watching television.

"You know I can't cancel at the last minute," I say.

"We're married now," he says. "We have to make time for each other." He makes a good point. When you marry, your life isn't your own anymore. You share it with your spouse. And if you don't put your marriage first, it won't become that steady foundation on which you can build the rest of your life. I realize that I have to decide what is important to me: Soccer? Girls' night? Touch football? Or my marriage? Sometimes I forget that Matt needs time with me just as I need time with him. And, in marriage, his problems are mine, and mine are his. So, if he sees my overbooked schedule as a problem, then I need to address it.

Do other newlyweds feel their separate interests, separate jobs, and separate friends are causing them and their husbands to live parallel lives? Matt and I have established some marital rituals to help us feel more connected throughout the week, like attending church on Sunday mornings and breakfasting afterwards, as well as kissing each other upon leaving for work or returning home. But what we lack is quality time together, which can be detrimental to a new marriage.

And the truth is I am starting to miss Matt. Even when he is home, we barely have enough time to exchange more than ten words in our rush to get ready for work each morning. When he returns home at night, half the time I'm in bed or at least dressing for it. On those nights that he does manage to escape from the office early he totes work home with him. And so lately I've found myself turning away from our marriage toward activities like soccer to make up for the loneliness I feel in it. But how can we ever build our marriage if we don't commit to spending time together?

I let Matt convince me to skip soccer that night. As I walk over to the gym, I try to push the thought of my team playing short a woman, thereby leaving one of our opponent's players wide open, out of my mind. After our workout, we regroup in the restaurant. It's dim in here, with most of its lighting coming from tea light candles. With my hand I cover one of the candles to feel its warmth as Matt orders sushi and a Japanese beer. He loves to try ethnic beers. His adventurous side doesn't get fulfilled by driving the same route to work every day, so he'll take change and experimentation wherever he can get it.

After the waiter walks away, our conversation begins. "I don't want to run my life on your schedule," I say, frustrated that I have to drop my plans for him. He needs to adjust his lifestyle, too.

"You shouldn't feel that way," he agrees. "But it concerns me that you don't want to put our time together first."

How could he have misinterpreted my actions? Of course,

he's my priority. "It's not that I wouldn't love to spend more time with you," I say, reaching for his hand. "It's just that I have other commitments in my life, too."

We know we must slow down our lives to find the time to strengthen our marital bond. But how do you do that? Matt pledges to delegate more tasks and trips to younger associates at work, and to sign up for one of my soccer teams. I promise to quit one of my soccer teams and enroll in classes that are more forgiving of an absence. And we agree to eat dinner together at least two nights a week.

But our new pace of life feels painfully slow. At home with Matt, I'm impatient, thinking of how my soccer team's performing in the play-offs. His mind wanders off, too, as he questions whether he should be spending more time at the office or bringing more work home with him. Soon, we revert back to some of our old habits. We know that eventually we'll need to adjust to the slower pace of life that marriage requires. But, for now, we'll live part of our lives in parallel.

TWENTY

An Attitude Adjustment: Should You Change?

Change your opinions, keep to your principles;
change your leaves, keep intact your roots.
−Victor Hugo

"I hate my job," I say to Matt, who is digging pulp out of a grapefruit while reading the newspaper at the kitchen table. It's early in the morning, and I'm tired. "I want to be a writer."

"Then you should do something about it," Matt says. Sometimes I get annoyed by how practical he is, how he offers up easy solutions, although admittedly, that's what attracts me to him, too. He tells me to visit a relative of his, Al, who I've never met before, because he writes a column for a local newspaper.

"How will that change anything?" I ask, because I spent ten years writing one novel that I failed to get published. How can Al change that?

"Stop being so afraid of people," Matt says, as he takes a sip of milk.

"I'm not afraid of people," I say defensively, but he's right.

While I'm an extrovert when I know people, I can be introverted when I don't. It bothers me that he sees my aversion to people as a weakness, that he forces me to see it as a flaw. I've learned to compensate for my fear. At parties, I sip water and, with my fingers, retrieve the floating lemon to chew on it while Matt talks. I let him draw me into the conversation, but he encourages me to be less dependent on him.

"Do you realize how much your fear of people limits you?" he asks, and, of course, I do. He says he wants others to see in me what he does, and they can't if I stay silent. Matt tells me if you're not improving yourself, you're declining. He compares it to how your muscles and circulatory system degenerate without exercise.

"He'd love to meet you," Matt adds, and that helps alleviate some of my fear. I realize my fear isn't so much of Al, but how he will perceive me.

Do other wives find their husbands objecting to some of their personality traits? If so, do they think they should change? And how do they determine which traits are inherently theirs, essential to their very being, and which are peripheral and can be changed?

Lately, I've been unhappy within our relationship, but I'm starting to realize that what's really bothering me is my life situation—that is, my job. What I've told Matt, that I hate my job, isn't true. I do like it. But what weighs on me is that I'll never feel content spending my life as a programmer. So, for the sake of our relationship, I need to root out the source of this negative energy in me. I can't just sit back and complain about how unfair life is; I have to take control of my destiny and start working toward my goal. And so, as hard as it is for me, I call Al. As Matt always says, nothing is gained without risk. Without risks, how far will you go in life?

As I drive to Al's house, I purposely take a wrong turn to try to convince myself that I am lost. When I arrive, he leads me to the living room, where he sits down in a high-backed chair. I stir cream into my coffee, pretending to concentrate on the vanishing white lines of cream so that I don't have to speak first.

"So, you want to be a writer?" Al says. I nod. He doesn't speak much more than I do, but he knows how to guide the conversation. "Why don't you try writing a column?"

I look at him blankly because I know nothing; I have no advice for others. "About what?"

"About what you know." He sees I'm still puzzled. "You know what it's like to move from New York to Minnesota. You know what it's like to be married." He hands me a book of columns that he self-published. "Write what you know."

I go home and write a column. The words come out easily, and it sells.

"Networking pays off," Matt says, because I am one step closer to becoming a writer, but I shrug him off.

I've always equated networking with asking for favors from people you don't know, but, as Matt has demonstrated, it's about more than that. It's about that spark your interaction discloses, which your insularity won't.

While I cried over boys in high school, my mom said, "Never change for a man." And she was right. You can't make somebody love you by changing who you are. But what if that person already does love you? And what if their changes make you a better, healthier person? Should you reject any changes outright, or should you listen and think about what they have said first? The truth is by listening to Matt I have developed the confidence I need to pursue my dream. And I'm starting to realize that you can't be a rigid thinker in marriage, stuck in your ways, when everything you do affects your spouse.

Four months after I met Al, he died of cancer. Matt held my hand as we walked into the funeral parlor. Al's son gave the homily. He said that while his father was dying, he asked to have his wife at his side. Matt squeezed my hand.

I knew then that I would change for Matt. He gives me the strength to turn to face my fears, and, through that, I grow.

TWENTY-ONE

The Mother-in-Law

Trust one who has gone through it.
—Virgil

*M*att's parents are driving down from Fargo to stay with us for the weekend. For some reason, I always feel stressed before his mom visits us. I worry that my house won't be clean enough, that she'll see the lint stuck in the vents or the fingerprints smearing our television screen or the dirt on the windowsill. I worry that she'll think I'm not taking good enough care of her son because I'm not the best cook. But, most of all, I worry that her presence will shift our family dynamics, that she'll be in charge and I'll have to defer to her because Matt does, only I'm not her child. And I'm not used to her style of parenting.

I know that as far as mothers-in-law go, I'm lucky. She doesn't make the sort of demands on us that would tear our marriage apart before we have a chance to begin building our life together. She doesn't pop in, take sides with her son, or attempt to run our marriage or our home. She expects us to build a life that is separate from hers. And she is a good person, always trying to do what is right and fair, with an optimistic view on life. My difficulty with her is more my uncertainty, my feeling of insecurity or incompetence that many newlyweds get from trying too hard to be a "good wife." And, in my case, it started with nothing more than pots and pans.

Before the wedding, Matt's mom and his sister, Liz, said, "Don't buy the heavy pots. You'll get tired of lifting them, plus you can't put them in the dishwasher." I wanted the heavy pots; I liked how they conducted heat. And, if I was to learn to cook, I'd learn to cook as an art form, which seemed to necessitate heavy pots. But now I was concerned. Would I offend them if I bought the heavy pots? I was afraid to risk their hurt and disappointment by disagreeing with them.

Then his sister Ann said, "Buy the heavy pots. They're good for cooking." Great. Now I had one Samuel vote for the heavy pots and two for the lighter ones. No matter which pots I chose, I'd offend at least one member of the Samuel family.

"They're pots!" I said later to Matt. "Why does everybody keep telling me which ones I should buy?" Because I felt caught between what I wanted and what his family recommended I buy. I felt caught between his mom and his sister, Liz, and his sister, Ann. Would buying the heavy pots strain my relationship with his mom and Liz? Would they think I was siding with one part of the family over the other?

But Matt couldn't see my point. "If you want the heavy pots, then get them," Matt said, exasperated. "Nobody cares which pots you buy. They're just giving you their opinion. They're only making conversation." But my family only gives advice when it's solicited. To hear his family's opinions expressed so frequently and so freely made me worry that they thought I was making poor choices.

"Jennifer, I don't want you to be a round peg that fits in a round hole. I want you to be the square peg that you are," Matt says, and I appreciate his support. While it is his job to run interference when necessary, I know that it is unfair for me to ask him to choose sides between his family, whom he has loved unconditionally for years, and me. But he endears me to him by being my biggest ally, as a spouse should be.

Next thing I knew, there I was at Marshall Field's, proclaiming my independence by selecting cast-iron pots heavy enough to double as dumbbells. I would not spend my life living under Matt's mom's thumb. And while I knew my reaction was not entirely rational—she probably hadn't given the pots a second thought after she left our house—I needed to make it clear that I was capable of making my own good decisions. I took my cookware home and set my five-piece set on the kitchen counter. Each piece was thick and dull and heavy and beautiful. That night, I boiled potatoes in the stockpot and charred meat in my frying pan and sautéed carrots in my saucepan. I'll admit I found it difficult to carry the stockpot while it was full of water. I had to lift it with two hands and felt as if I had weights tied to my fingertips. When I tipped the pot over the sink to pour the water out slowly, it all came sloshing out, and one of the smaller potatoes slipped down the garbage disposal. Plus, the water splashed up and out of the sink, soaking the bottom of my shirt. But I didn't mention that to Matt.

"I'll wash the pots and pans while you clear," I said to Matt after dinner. He agreed. I filled the sink with soapy water. He cleared the dinner table, setting the plates, glasses, and utensils in the dishwasher. Then he put the A.1. sauce and salad dressing back into the refrigerator and wiped the table clean.

"Do you need help, dear?" he asked, wiping his hands off on a kitchen towel.

"No, thanks," I said cheerfully, still scrubbing at the sink. I was feeling optimistic; I had already cleaned three lids and the stockpot, including the potato juice that had boiled over the side of it. And so he left the kitchen to work in the office for a while. I stood there and began scrubbing the frying pan. I scrubbed and I scrubbed and I scrubbed. Soon, my feet started to itch from standing there for so long. I doused the pan with Comet and switched to a brillo pad to try to get rid of the dried food burned into the pan. While the pan was great for browning meat, it wasn't as easy to clean as I had hoped. I found it impossible to get all of the burnt food up, and so I filled the pan with water and let it soak overnight.

"Weren't you going to wash that pan?" Matt asked when he came back into the kitchen. He likes the sink area clean. I explained that I had to let the pan soak, and he looked perplexed but nodded. And then I realized that his mom was right. I hate my pots and pans. Life would have been so much easier if I had bought cookware that I could stick in the dishwasher. And now I'm afraid that she'll realize how right she was and reclaim her turf during her next visit.

That weekend, Matt's mom arrives with a pan of lasagna that she made for us. Together we go into the kitchen to heat it up and make a salad. While we work together, I wait for her to ask me if I like my new pots even though I can barely lift them or why I bought them when she recommended against the purchase. But she never follows up to make sure that I've taken her advice. In fact, I don't think she even notices that I didn't. And that conveys to me that she respects the decisions that I make.

I start to pay attention to how she gives advice. She doesn't preface it with, "Do it this way," but "What works for me is . . ." Through her careful choice of wording she gives me the option to take or leave her advice. And then I understand that Matt was right: she is just giving her opinion. If I constantly set her up for failure, she can't win. After breaking all of my nails while scrubbing those pots and pans fifty times over, I'll admit that often she does have good advice.

Slowly, I'm learning to trust Matt's mom, and she is opening up to me. She confesses that as a newlywed she was clueless as to how to run her household, and shares stories about how she burned bread, accidentally forgot to cook a chicken before serving it, and turned her husband's socks and undershirts pink in the washing machine. That comes as a surprise to me, as she always seems so efficient in the kitchen and can make a full meal from leftovers, completely different from the original one, so that you don't even know you're eating the same dish as the night before. "It took years of practice," she says. I'm discovering that she's not so different than I am; she didn't fall into her marriage knowing who she was. She learned just as I am learning, through trial and error.

And then I realize that I'm not in competition with her. Our families should be part of where Matt and I derive our strength.

TWENTY-TWO

The Draft

Him that I love, I wish to be free—even from me.
—Anne Morrow Lindbergh

𝓘 hate fantasy football and whoever invented it. Every Sunday morning, the phone rings off the hook. And I know that it's Keith or Greg or John calling to trade a wide receiver, a tight end, or a quarterback with Matt.

"Will you get that?" Matt yells, holed up in the office, searching the Internet for sleeper player picks and team rankings and rumors.

I bring the cordless phone to him. "I don't answer the phone on Sundays," I say and walk out. The phone will ring all afternoon—after each interception, touchdown, and tackle—and into the evening as the guys tally their scores. I cannot understand why they are so competitive. You'd think they were the twelfth man on the field.

It all started with the draft. Matt had offered to host it in our downstairs family room. He had spent weeks combing through magazines to plan his player picks, and I was starting to feel a bit left out. So I decided to take a little more interest in football to share his hobby with him. Since their fantasy football league has a strict "no girls" policy, I'd be his silent partner. I remembered the names of the quarterbacks and figured out what a tight end was—the position Matt used to play in high school. I made a few rules for myself for the season, which I knew Matt would appreciate: conversations only during commercials; cheer when his player intercepts a pass or scores a touchdown; remember which color team you're rooting for. And, on the day of the draft, I bubbled over with the anticipation of what his final player lineup would be. That night, he'd draft fifteen players from NFL teams, skill position players who caught passes, rushed for yardage, and scored touchdowns. Each week he'd compete against one of his fantasy football pal's teams, earning points based on his skill players' performances. And if he won enough games in regular season to place in the top half of his league, he'd make the playoffs. "Would you like me to make appetizers for you guys?" I asked.

"No, thanks," Matt said. "We usually order pizza and drink beer." He had on his purple Vikings jersey. *Do you realize that you're not a professional football player?* I wanted to ask. He looked like a meathead.

I was shocked by the noise generated by the twelve men downstairs. Their hoots and hollers, claps and stamps, snorts and laughs reverberated through the house as they drafted players and set their season's schedule. I realized that the draft was at our house not because we had the most space but because the women who were married longer knew better. I shut every door between the guys and me and called Brenda. She could hear them through the phone.

The next morning, I went downstairs to find pizza boxes and beer bottles and huge white sheets of paper with names scribbled on them taped to our family room wall. "You have got to be kidding me," I said to myself, thinking, *This must be what it's like to wake up in a frat house*. Matt came downstairs then and started bagging up the beer bottles, but he asked that we leave the draft picks hanging on the walls.

"I got my top choice for a first-round pick," he said proudly, and I reminded myself to be supportive. I was not going to complain about the mess. I didn't want to be one of those unsupportive wives who keep their husband on a tight leash. I wanted to be one of the cool ones who's looked at as one of the guys. Besides, it was just for one night, wasn't it?

But, of course, it wasn't. The draft required subscribing to the NFL Sunday package and ESPN Insider. It required frantic Internet research on Sunday mornings to determine which eight players he should start with and then again on Monday nights to check the scores. It required a beautiful afternoon to be wasted in front of the television. And, no matter where I went in the house, I could hear Matt yelling at the television. *Do you realize that you're not the coach? Those players on television can't hear you, and, even if they could, they wouldn't take your advice*, I wanted to yell back. Then I realized that that was the point of fantasy football. On Sundays, Matt and his friends could be the players and the coaches. They could be whoever they wanted to be.

One Sunday I walked downstairs and sat next to Matt on the couch. I watched as the players bashed into one another, knocking each other to the ground. "Don't you think watching football is a waste of your time?" I asked, but he barely heard me. Sometimes I think whatever Matt is focused on becomes physically attached to him; it's that hard to pry his eyes from it. So I repeated myself and got a "Huh?"

"We should be spending today together," I said. "It's beautiful out. Let's go for a walk."

"Jennifer, if I win the pool, you can keep the earnings," he said. And then his attention went back to the television set. Winnings? That made me think fantasy football was even more of a waste. I'm not a gambler. At casinos, I head straight for the nickel slots, while Matt plunks down a hundred bucks at the blackjack table. If I win, I'm so thankful that I didn't lose that I can't enjoy my earnings.

I suppose that Matt should keep some of his single habits, even those I don't understand. And I'm starting to realize that fantasy football provides Matt with his much-needed downtime. If fantasy football relaxes him and gives him enjoyment, then I will support him in pursuing it. He has a right to choose how he wants to spend his free time.

And honestly, I'm starting to realize that we don't need to spend every minute together to feel secure in our marriage. It's okay to live parts of your life outside your couple domain. You'll come back to each other with new interests and more to talk about. If Matt wants to watch football at Keith or Greg or John's house, he's welcome to go alone. I don't want to suffocate him.

But I do need time with him, too, so while he's watching a football game I negotiate with him: If you plan to spend the afternoon watching football, then you need to spend the morning with me. He nods his head. I'm not sure if he's agreeing with me or showing his enthusiasm for a catch that was just made, but I leave the room anyway.

Matt wins the season. A two-foot trophy, with his team name—The Thundering Herd, after his alma mater—engraved on it arrives at our home. He places it on top of our entertainment center for us to share in his victory all year round. Along with the trophy comes a check—and the end of football season. And I'm not sure which brings a bigger smile to my face.

TWENTY-THREE

The Nest Egg

*The only way not to think about money is to have a
great deal of it.*
—Edith Wharton

I opened my mail to find a bank statement for a savings account, as well as stocks, from my mom. She had enclosed a
note. *"Remember all of those sodas I refused to buy you when
you were a child? Here's where the money went."* I had to laugh.
The savings account had grown to several hundred dollars, and
the stocks were worth much more.

When I called my mom to thank her, she said, "You may want
to keep this money separate from your marital assets. When
women my age married, we kept what we called a nest egg,
where we stashed money in case anything went wrong down the
road." She tells me about some of the risks in life and marriage
that she's seen: divorce, desertion, disablement, and death. If
you're financially dependent on your husband, then how do you
survive these life transitions?

This is typical of my mom. She's always encouraged me to
keep my own money, "just in case." Before I left for dates while

in high school, she'd tuck a quarter in my pocket "just in case it goes sour." To her, money represents freedom and independence, power and control.

But is it fair to have your own money in marriage? Is this simply practical advice with over half of all marriages ending in divorce? Or is having your own money in marriage an act of bad faith?

I'll admit that I've thought long and hard about hiding money from Matt, about stashing a little from each paycheck that comes in, not a noticeable amount but enough to provide a safety cushion in years to come. A nest egg would provide me with that emotional comfort and security I crave, a reserve of funds into which I can dip in case of some emergency.

Since the beginning of time, women have been hiding money from their husbands in nest eggs. What is at the core of this time-honored tradition? Is it merely a lesson passed from one generation to the next? Or throughout history has it been a necessity? Today, does it simply fulfill some inner need for emotional security?

My grandmother kept a nest egg in a piggy bank out of necessity. Her husband never knew about it. She married during World War II and learned to respect money. She saved money for her nest egg any way she could: by cutting and styling her children's hair; by making clothes out of the printed material in which the chicken feed would come; by using the soft breast feathers from chickens she'd pluck to stuff the quilts and pillows. No purchase was made at the grocery store that could be raised at home—like chickens—or grown in the garden, like vegetables and fruits, which she canned for winter. Neither she nor her husband threw away anything they thought they could reuse, such as material scraps for colorful quilts and orange rinds for breads and cookies.

She didn't believe in layaway, insisting you went without until you had saved enough money to purchase what you wanted.

She'd use her nest egg for special occasions, like a new shirt or pants for her husband on his birthday. "Keep any money you make before you marry in your maiden name," she told my mom. But it was only after the death of her husband that she realized the true value of her nest egg. The banks froze all of the money that was held in both her and her husband's name while his estate was being settled. Fortunately, she had saved enough money to buy groceries, gas, and utilities for six months.

Through my grandmother, my mom realized the importance of having a nest egg, but she had another reason for keeping hers. She stopped working shortly after she married my dad and quickly discovered that she didn't like having to ask him for money. My mom and dad enjoy money differently. My mom enjoys what she spends, and my dad enjoys what he does not. He wants every penny accounted for, and thinks spending money on new curtains, a dinette set, or fabric is frivolous. She tired of him constantly questioning her spending habits.

Shortly thereafter, my dad agreed to let her control the family finances. At that point, she began to save wherever she could to build her own nest egg: she dried the laundry outdoors in the summer and over the hot air ducts in the winter; she cut coupons and used them on each trip to the grocery store; she set the thermostat low. She repaired toilets, windows, and whatever else she could. As her nest egg grew, she began investing in stocks and bonds.

There was a definite shift, a time when the fear set in, when she saw what happened when women her age were traded in for trophy wives half their age. These women, who had always trusted their husbands, suddenly found themselves forced to take care of themselves and their children. With less education and work experience than their professional husbands, they scrambled to get low-income jobs to support their children, while the men, financially set, continued on with their lives. She wondered what would happen to herself and her children if she ever found herself in a similar position. She decided that there were two things a woman needed in life: her own money and an education. She began to see her nest egg as marriage insurance, sort of like disability insurance—you hope you never have to use it, but you know you'll be taken care of if you do. And she used part of her nest egg to go back to college.

While her fear has given me my own fear, it has also given me a strength I'm not sure I'd have otherwise. She made education a priority for all four of us: My oldest sister, Christina, with one child, a dog, and a cat, is wading through a Ph.D. program at Johns Hopkins; my younger sister, Suzanne, is pursuing fashion at Parsons School of Design; and my youngest sister, Cassandra, has just graduated from college and moved to New York City to start her career.

And now, looking down at the financial documents in my hand, I debate whether I should tell Matt about the money my mom has saved for me. To not tell him seems like a betrayal to him, but to tell him seems like a betrayal to my mom, who has worked hard over the years to get my nest egg started. And so I leave the bank and stock statements on the dining room table until he notices them. He reads through them and smiles. "That was nice of your mom," he says, and that's it. He doesn't mention making the money joint, and so I don't either.

When Matt and I first married, I paid little attention to our finances. I'm not a money person. I didn't care which funds he put our money into, and I trusted that he'd invest well. I've always admired how generous Matt is with his earnings. He insisted both of our names appear on all of our assets, including those with which he came into our marriage, in case something should happen to him. And a prenuptial agreement was never mentioned. But still, a part of me—a part of him, perhaps, too—realizes that by crediting him for being generous with his money, I'm acknowledging that it is his money. And isn't diversification what smart financial planning is all about? I believe everybody needs some money that is his or her own, whether they've earned it or inherited it. Without that power, how do you control your life or make decisions surrounding it? Money is freedom. I'd never want to have to stay in a marriage simply because I couldn't afford to get out of it.

I have some financial independence now, with my own paycheck and my faithful contribution to a 401(k) plan. But what worries me is what will happen if I decide to quit my job or reduce my hours to care for our future children. I'm starting to wonder if I should reconsider my role in our finances now, to plan for not only our future but mine as well. Statistically, women live longer than men do. Chances are I'll outlive Matt. And, as much as I hate to admit it, I do hear a tiny voice in my head that asks me what I'll do if our marriage doesn't work out. How will I support myself if I've left the workforce to raise our children? And Matt has more earning potential than I do. He is a partner at his law firm and his salary should go up each year. If I take time out of the workforce, I'll likely never recoup my wage losses. That means I won't contribute money toward Social Security or my 401(k) plan, and, upon reentering the workforce, I'll probably earn less than I would have had I kept working.

I trust Matt to do what is right and to be fair. But sometimes life choices aren't that black and white. What you consider fair isn't necessarily what your spouse considers fair, and your instinct is to protect yourself first. Maybe twenty years down the road he will leave or I will or maybe he will die or I will. You can't always control your future or the obstacles you find in it. Marriage can be hard and tiring, and, after twenty years of it, who's to say that Matt and I won't find it exhausting and look for an easier alternative? There is something unpredictable in being human. We're not always in control of ourselves. So, for me, this nest egg isn't about trust. It's about that worry that life may take you in a direction you don't want to go, one in which you can't control. But can you keep one foot in a marriage, and your other foot out of it? Or with today's divorce rate must you simply protect yourself?

I can't decide what is right, so I leave the money sitting in my account in Ithaca. I tell myself that closing the account or trying to make it joint would be more of a pain than it's worth, but I wonder if that is really true. Perhaps I do need a nest egg more than I realize.

TWENTY-FOUR

My Career or Yours?

I have spread my dreams under your feet;
Tread softly because you tread on my dreams.
—William Butler Yeats

On Monday morning I awake with my head abuzz. I have tight deadlines at work, plus what feels like an endless list of personal phone calls to make before noon. As a first-time home owner, I'm surprised by how much work is required to manage our home. I need to get bids for reinsulating our attic, installing a runner on our foyer stairs, and reupholstering the couch. And I don't have an office door that I can shut to make these calls. Whatever I say on the phone from within my cubicle is heard throughout the department.

And on Wednesday, either Matt or I need to be home to let in the cable installer. This has sparked a debate between us.

"If I stay home, then I'll have to work later to make up my billable hours," he says. Matt's job is more demanding and stressful and requires more hours than mine does.

"But if I stay home, I'll have to take a vacation day," I argue. I'm a clock puncher; my job has little flexibility. And I don't want to negotiate for more time off. At the moment, I feel insecure at work. Our company is making that uncomfortable shift from a small organization to a larger one, and you can feel the uncertainty at every level.

My manager quit the day before my wedding, and so I am temporarily reporting to Brian, our group president. Brian is known for being everywhere at once. He controls a portfolio of companies and still finds time to review my documentation and database designs. And he's not your typical MBA IT manager. In addition to that MBA, he's a self-taught programmer, so you actually have to do the work. You can't overload him with acronyms or technical jargon to get an approving—if somewhat befuddled—nod. And he's as demanding as Matt is. He will not tolerate work that isn't thorough or well done. He knows that one flaw in the technical design can cost the company hundreds of thousands of dollars to correct, and so he micromanages larger projects. Plus, he shares Matt's relentless energy, for which he expects you to keep pace.

Working for Brian makes me feel as if I finally have a chance to prove myself. And my career, no matter how much I complain about it, is important to me. I am goal oriented, eager to advance, and personally identify with my career, just as Matt does with his. But right now, I feel sloppy and run down, pressured at work with an inflexible schedule while trying to keep up with the demands of running our household.

So Matt and I are discovering the curse of the dual career couple: What do you put first, your family or your career? As a modern woman in a modern marriage, I wonder if your marriage makes your life stronger, your direction clearer, or does it get hopelessly muddled as you try to do it all? Obviously, love will not pay the bills. And while Matt says he believes that our marriage comes first, I feel that he puts it second to his career. A marriage is about protecting your spouse's self-worth and self-esteem. And my self-esteem and self-worth aren't building while I'm pushing a cart through Target in search of toilet paper or peeking into an egg carton to ensure nothing within is broken; it builds when I'm somehow improving myself, like using my mind to help design a software program at work. While I know all of these tasks are necessary to keep a household running smoothly, I need to feel that Matt values my career, too. I feel as if I'm being forced to choose between work and family—and because Matt makes more money than I do, I'm forced to choose family while he chooses work.

Anne feels as if her career is starting to come second, too. As a sales representative, she works from home. She is one of the most driven people I have ever met. Currently, she and Pete live in a town house, but they are looking to buy a house of their own. They are trying to get a preapproved mortgage. Anne can't stand their mortgage broker, and so she asked Pete to deal with him. And it was Pete, with his need to line-edit contracts—which Anne readily signed—who had all of the questions. But while at work Pete rarely answers the telephone. Like Matt, he works with billable hours, and so he doesn't like to take calls that interrupt him. Since Anne perceives a ringing phone as a potential sale, and therefore money, she always answers promptly. Whenever the mortgage broker couldn't reach Pete, he'd call Anne, as he knew he could always get in touch with her. She'd tell him to call Pete, and then she'd call Pete herself to tell him to answer his phone, but sometimes neither of them could get through, and then the mortgage broker would call her again.

Fielding Pete's telephone calls became an internal struggle for Anne. She needed to feel that her career was important, too, and so she'd e-mail Pete little reminders. *"My time is just as valuable as yours."* Or, *"I'm not your secretary."* I know how she feels.

Brenda has a different challenge. Her career automatically comes first in her household, as she makes more money than Mike does and carries their medical insurance. She works as an IT analyst while he is employed as a painter. And knowing that she can never quit her job is difficult for her. She'd eventually like to be a stay-at-home mom, but with Mike having to pay child support, his salary alone would not support the lifestyle they choose.

Matt and I appreciate the benefits of having a double income, too—living in a neighborhood of our choosing, vacationing in prime spots, not having to be as frugal as we would on a single income. But working long hours means we both return home tired at the end of the day. Often our mood depends on what type of day we had. Tension that begins at the office sometimes spills over into conflicts we have at home. Both of us need our downtime at the end of the day to relax and unwind. But this remodeling project, with all of the tasks and demands that go with it, prevents us from getting it. And we still haven't decided who should stay home on Wednesday to meet the cable installer.

"I feel like you think your career is more important than mine," I say.

"I don't think that my career is more important than yours," Matt says. "But I do make more than you. Don't you think it makes sense for my career to come first? That will maximize our earning potential as a couple." He says this with no malice. To him, this decision is a simple mathematical formula. For years, Matt has worked with a financial adviser on a plan to allow him to retire comfortably at fifty-five. All of his monetary decisions have kept this goal in mind. Obviously, my income alone would not let us reach this goal. But currency comes in many different forms. I don't want my lower earning potential to penalize me in our marriage, to relegate me to a support role.

For him, part of being a good husband is about supporting his family financially. And he enjoys that psychological satisfaction he derives from working hard. But while you may clearly see the results you get from working hard professionally—a promotion, a paycheck, a corner office—the rewards you get from the efforts you put into your marriage aren't always as evident. And you don't want to give your best energy to your career at the expense of your marriage. You need to support your spouse's dreams and goals. You can't pursue your own at his or her expense.

Finally, I resentfully agree to stay home. Matt's presented a more convincing argument than I have. But he does concede that our marriage—and true intimacy—will only work if we are equals in it, and being equal requires shared responsibility. By cooperating, we can lessen the strain our remodeling project has put on our marriage. Matt agrees to take some of the tasks to which he's assigned me to work with him. At lunch, he shuts his office door to make the phone calls they require. Sometimes, he stops at the grocery store or dry cleaner on his way home from work. And he always helps clear the table after dinner. I appreciate his consideration for my feelings. I feel better knowing that we're a little bit closer to sharing the household tasks and the pressure of working full-time equally, although I know that we'll revisit this issue often. We still have a long way to go to make our division of labor fair.

TWENTY-FIVE

Eat Less, Live Longer

Who does not grow, declines.
—Rabbi Hillel

re you sure you want to eat that?" Matt asks, and I glare at him. He isn't concerned that I'm gaining weight; he's worried that I'm clogging my arteries and reducing my life span. Recently, he read a report on CNN.com that stated studies have shown you extend your life span by reducing your caloric intake. Unlike me, a sucker for instant gratification, Matt always plans for the future. If eating less now will add ten healthy years onto our lives, then he wants to try it. Matt loves life. I put down my cheeseburger out of guilt.

I love food. I love to eat a lot of it in one sitting, like a half bag of chips in front of the television. With my horrible eating habits, I am your stereotypical American. Take me to a French restaurant and, in addition to my meal, I'll eat all of the bread in the basket to ensure I feel full. I eat hot dogs without worrying what's in them and lick my fingers clean after I've finished off a small bag of Cheetos. And I eat so quickly that sometimes I have to remind myself to put my fork down between bites and breathe.

During our engagement period, I joined Weight Watchers, and, for the first time ever, discovered portion control. Every day, I logged into Weight Watchers' Web site to track what I ate. And I was astonished by how much I ate. On one day I exceeded my point intake by fifty points, about twice the calories a person of my height and weight should consume. As a bride-to-be, I managed to lose ten pounds in several hungry and grumpy weeks by plowing through five-pound bags of carrots with fat-free bean dip. Once our wedding day passed I gave in to my chocolate and salt cravings and reverted back to some of my old eating habits. Only now Matt—who, at six foot two and 215 pounds, used to like to eat as much as I did—is on a health kick. But when we first married, he ate so much on nights that he went jogging that I took to hiding some of my junk food from him behind the cereal boxes in the pantry. One day, he found it.

"What's this?" he asked. It was a bag of cheese popcorn, one of my favorite snacks.

"Just something I picked up on my way home," I lied. I had had it for a few days now.

"Do you hide food from me?" Matt asked incredulously. "You do, don't you? We can't hide food from each other!" And I felt badly then for my dishonesty until he opened up the bag and started to eat big handfuls of *my* cheese popcorn. Am I a bad person for not wanting to share my food?

But now, here is Matt telling me that whenever we go out for dinner we should split a plate of food; at home we should switch to organic fruits and antibiotic-free meats and pop a vitamin each day; and that we should cut back on the amount of canned tuna we eat because of its possible mercury contamination levels.

I don't mind splitting a meal at T.G.I. Friday's, where the servings are so huge that fries tumble off your plate. But at restaurants with smaller portions, where the meat sits over the mashed potatoes and practically hides them from view, I know what splitting a plate with Matt means. His bite is three times mine, so I end up with a third of what's served, which isn't much to begin with. And while he insists that my stomach will gradually shrink and its caloric expectations will fade, right now it painfully grumbles.

So what do you do when your spouse isn't the same person with whom you walked down the aisle? Before Matt and I married, I heard repeatedly, "Don't expect your spouse to change." That, from my experience, is not true. I think you should expect your spouse to change, just not how you want him to. Have other wives noticed their husbands changing in ways they didn't anticipate?

Meanwhile, Anne has discovered that her real age, as calculated by a health Web site, is greater than her actual age. "How can I be older than I am?" she asks, stunned. "I'm not overweight. I have none of the risk factors." She admits that she lived off McDonald's and Burger King in college and hates to exercise. And so on her notepad she jotted down all of the vitamins the Web site recommends she take.

Already, she's been trying to make Pete and her lifestyle healthier. Like Matt, she plans for the future and knows that caring for their bodies now will help them live a long, healthy life. And she's a bit of a germaphobe. After hearing about traces of feces that appear on money, she started keeping wipes in her glove compartment so that she could wipe germs from her hands after being handed money when going through a drive-through. When she and Pete were dating, she convinced him to stop smoking, although she said even today he'd lick an ashtray if given the chance. And shortly after they married, she started them on the Zone Diet. Not for her; she is thin and lanky, but for him. A self-described Russian bear because of his heritage and barrel chest, he admits he could lose a few pounds.

So to better their health, she bought jugs of vitamins like vitamin E and calcium from Costco and a plastic one-a-day pill case from Target. "I'm the a.m.—*A* for *Anne*—and you're the p.m.—*P* for *Pete*," she said as she laid out their pills for the week. She told him the health benefit of each one.

He looked down at the pill case as if it contained cyanide. "I'll choke on those horse pills," he said. She took all of the pills out of the case and cut them in half. He looked at her, down at the pills, and started taking them.

In life, there is one constant, and that is change. And change is good, as it encourages progress. Your spouse, like you, is constantly evolving and won't always be the same person you agreed to marry at the altar. So, for Matt's sake, I try to become a healthier eater, knowing that a shared goal will help us grow closer.

A few weeks later, I've overcome the discomfort that is caused when you're pushed beyond your comfort zone. The stomach rumbling has stopped, and, not only have I adjusted to smaller portion sizes, but I've lost weight and gained energy, too. And, while uncomfortable at first, I've come to like the changes in Matt and myself.

TWENTY-SIX

The Housecleaner: What Makes a "Good Wife"?

Nothing can bring you peace but yourself.
—Ralph Waldo Emerson

*H*ere I am on a Saturday afternoon cleaning our home. I've spent three hours following my scrub path from the kitchen to the storage room and now our floors shine like clear nail polish and I smell like lemons and Comet. As I wring out my mop, I realize that the feminist in me has suddenly embraced the traditional institution of marriage. I can spend an entire afternoon baking brownies for Matt, smoothing out the frosting with a thick butter knife until there are no chocolate waves left in it. Does that make me a hypocrite?

When Matt comes home from work, I smile at him from the top of the stairs. I'm impatient for him to come up to the landing to see how great I've made our house look. But he only climbs halfway up our black slate stairs before he stops and looks down. "Do you see that?" he asks. I see nothing, just the step beneath him, and think perhaps I have finally driven him over the edge. But then he leans over and wipes one of my dirty footprints from the stairs. And then another. And then one more. Watching him I realize I should have taken my shoes off at the door, but, after the work I've put in, I'm not ready to confess that to Matt. Instead, I think to myself that he probably gives himself credit for helping me clean today. I'm convinced that women underestimate the amount of work that they do around the house, while men overestimate theirs. But he sighs. "I think it's time we hire a housecleaner," he says.

"But I've been doing so well!" I say, surprised to find that his words sting. Why is it that I, the queen of the messies, have suddenly become territorial?

Obviously, Matt didn't fall in love with me because I could cook or clean. When your singleton motto is, "Don't learn how to cook or clean or it'll be your job for the rest of your life," you don't exactly develop domestic skills. So what if boiling corn required a call home or I broke my food processor by putting too many potatoes in it? If a button pops off a shirt, we can always pay a tailor to stitch it back on. I refused to spend hours laboring over monotonous, repetitive work that you can never get ahold of because any achievement is erased by a simple object the next morning: a dirty dish in the sink, a dirty shirt in the laundry basket, a muddy shoe tracking footprints. But, in marriage, somebody has to do these chores, and what do you do if your husband doesn't like to do them, either?

I thought I had solved that dilemma: I'd be responsible for the outdoor chores, while my husband took care of the traditionally female indoor ones. But then I discovered that I don't like how my fingers and toes numb when I shovel, or how autumn's draft slips beneath my pullover like cold hands when I rake, or how the mosquitoes bite me and the dirt and grass flies up from beneath the mower and sticks to my sweaty face when

I mow. The truth is I'm happier indoors where I have climate control.

And then, before I knew it, I found myself emulating my friend, Cindy, who does housework not because society expects it of her, but because there's something elegant and chic in keeping a Pottery Barn home with marinated meats in your refrigerator. I wanted to be like my mom was—a woman who planted flowers outdoors along the sidewalks, kept the house so clean you couldn't even find fingerprints in it, and had a healthy and delicious dinner, with all of the food groups represented, ready for her husband when he returned home from work. I wanted to be what I always dreaded becoming: a good wife, a congenial hostess, devoted to my husband.

I thought I was finally getting there, that I was finally starting to understand what my role was in our marriage and how I could contribute to our partnership. And now, here I am, fired. Not from my work as a programmer. There, I know what I'm doing— you tell me what you want and through technology I can achieve it. I'm fired from being a homemaker because I am utterly clueless as to how to make our household work.

And so I just stand there at the top of the steps, staring down at Matt who is looking at the dirt on his hand. "I know I'm not the best cleaner," I say, because admittedly I'm not. I'm too inconsistent, tackling our household chores on some days with zest, while other days it's as if the vacuum cleaner sucked up my energy along with the dirt. "But don't you think your expectations are a bit too high? And don't you think a housecleaner is a waste of money?"

Matt sighs. He comes up the stairs, and I follow him into the kitchen where he washes his hands. "Dear, do you really want to spend your Saturday afternoons cleaning?" he asks. And the weird thing is that I suddenly do. I want a shiny home that is the result of my sweat, my labor. But he convinces me to try a house-cleaner just once. Just once, he says. To be fair, I agree.

The truth is that this isn't about Matt. This isn't about the cleaner. It's about me and who I am and who I have become in marriage. I am having an identity crisis. Signing with my new name of Mrs. Samuel reminds me of that. To me, *Mrs.* implies I've been domesticated, which obviously isn't the case, while *Samuel* means that I belong to his family instead of mine. What I am supposed to be good at—cooking, cleaning, and organizing—I'm not, and what I am good at—creativity, athletics, and enthusiasm—doesn't seem to be of any value in our marriage. If I can't adapt to a traditional role, then what will make *me* a good wife? What will I contribute to our marriage?

And so I ask Brenda who cleans in their home. "I do," she sighs. "I have a different standard of cleanliness than Mike does. He doesn't notice dirt, anywhere. I don't think he knows where the vacuum is." In their household, Mike is responsible for the outdoor chores. But outdoor chores, like mowing the lawn or shoveling the sidewalks, are seasonal and performed infrequently. So, once in a while, she'd like some help with the daily indoor chores. As she doesn't feel right nagging Mike to pitch in, she tries to lead by example. She hopes that by watching her clean he'll eventually start sweeping the kitchen floor or folding the laundry, rather than stepping over it. And she has begun to do what Mike calls "four-point vacuuming." While he's watching television, she'll plant herself directly in his line of vision, and then vacuum as slowly as possible, rotating her body a few degrees after a couple strokes in each direction, all the while blocking his view of the screen.

I'm not like Brenda. Like Mike, I don't notice dirt. And so I ask Anne, who actually enjoys cleaning, if she knows who she is in marriage, or if she feels just as confused as I do. "I feel comfortable with who I am in our marriage," she says. "I am the household organizer. I'm responsible for identifying what needs to be done, and making sure it gets done. I can't cook or decorate, and I don't care." Her scripting for what it means to be a good wife came from her mom, who had a career outside the home. And Pete is more creative than Anne is. He can cook wonderful meals while she cringes at the thought of sticking her hand into the cavity of a turkey, and he can pull together any room using colors that she never knew matched. But what bothers Anne are the assumptions that other people make about her marriage, assuming she has a traditional role in it. Guests usually compliment her on dinner or her decorating style, when it was Pete who did all of the work.

"Nobody really has a traditional relationship," Anne says, "Even in the fifties, couples had their quirks. Everybody does what they can to be happy." She makes a good point. You can't judge people. What looks to be traditional isn't necessarily, and, even if it is, what does it matter, if both spouses are happy with the arrangement?

Pete is fine with his role and Anne's role in their marriage; Anne is fine with her role and Pete's role in their marriage. She says what's important isn't that you do what society expects of you, but that you do what works for you and your spouse. And so I decide to let go of my preconceived notions of what it means to be a good wife and follow Anne's example of finding my own path. That, of course, is not easy.

A week later, I come home to find that Sharon, the woman Matt has hired, has been there. Based on her work, she must be a perfectionist like Matt is. I imagine her attacking the lint on his bathroom rug as I attack a bag of salt and vinegar potato chips.

Everything on Matt's list, which he left on the counter for her, is crossed off: she vacuumed his bathroom rug, took all of his newspapers to the recycling bin in our garage, and cleaned out the refrigerator, tossing out bottles of salad dressing Matt had moved into our new home with. She even folded the edges of our toilet paper into a V shape. Looking around the house, I feel spoiled but delighted. And I have to admit that I'm glad we hired her—she has done a much better job than I ever would.

Matt walks through our front door like a general inspecting the barracks. He likes to slide his fingers along the clean, shiny surfaces. I swear he can hear dust settle. "The house looks great," he says, as he gets out of his business attire and into khaki pants and a loose-fitting button-down shirt.

By paying for a housecleaner, we have one less issue to argue over in our marriage. There are fewer fights about who should do what or how thoroughly it should be done. But I am left wondering what will make Matt and my partnership equal if I have nothing to contribute to it. What kind of wife am I?

TWENTY-SEVEN

Who's Right?

It is not who is right, but what is right,
that is important.
–Thomas Huxley

I'm desperately trying to shovel my car out of the snowbank at the end of our driveway. But its tires are jammed, and each time I press the accelerator, they sink deeper into the roadside slush. My neighbor, Kim, puts on her hat and gloves and comes over with a shovel, but still we can't free my car. I try Matt's cell phone, but he doesn't answer. I try his colleague Rick's cell phone, too, but again there is no answer. Finally, another neighbor gets out of his car and helps us push. At last, my car rocks forward and then rolls backward out of the slush.

Driving along 394, I realize that I am forty-five minutes late for dinner with Matt and Rick. The Timberwolves game, for which Matt and I have tickets, starts in less than one hour. So why hasn't Matt called? I could be lying facedown bleeding in the snow somewhere.

When I get to the restaurant, I see that two more colleagues have joined Matt, leaving no room for me at the four-person table. So I stand in the aisle, trying to make small talk, as the waiters rotate their trays to scoot by me. I glare at the back of Matt's head, willing him to offer up his seat. But he doesn't notice. I fume. Now I know that the reason he didn't call was that I wasn't on his mind, and that hurts. I excuse myself before I implode. "I have to go to the bookstore," I say, and Matt looks up at me curiously. He has a full beer in front of him that I know will take him forever to finish. "Why don't you join me after you finish your drink?"

"I'll be there in a minute," he says. He has no idea what sort of dialogue is going through my head.

Sitting in the bookstore's coffee shop, I sip on a hot brew, carefully planning what to say to Matt. I need to deliver my words with enough force to coerce him into seeing my point of view. I'm as tense and focused as a boxer preparing for a fight. I feel his hands on my shoulders before I see his face. He has entered the ring.

"Sit down," I say angrily. "I'm angry with you." He looks confused but takes a seat. "First of all, I was an hour late. An hour, Matt! Why didn't you try calling me to make sure that I was okay? I could have been in a car accident! I could have been lying on the roadside somewhere. And you didn't even save me a seat at the restaurant. How can you be so inconsiderate? Did you even realize that I wasn't there? Are you that selfish to think only of yourself? You need to start thinking about me, too!" I'm hot as a high-watt lightbulb. I have him against the ropes, amidst a flurry of punches.

Matt puts his hands up on the table and backs up his chair. "I should have given you my seat. For that I apologize. But you can't be upset with me for not calling you. You said that you were going to be late and to order dinner for you."

I forgot that I had told him that I needed to take a phone call. But I'm too livid to stop sparring now. The ten-second count has begun. It doesn't seem fair that Matt can hurt me and then get no punishment of his own. For me, this argument has become an act of self-preservation.

"I don't understand why you get so angry," Matt says. Hasn't he heard anything that I've said? What other emotion is there to feel aside from anger?

We walk over to the game then. I feel a million miles from him, but when he picks up my hand, my anger begins to dissipate. That gesture shows me that even though we may see things differently, he still cares. I can't help being amazed by how Matt is open and receptive to my feelings. Matt proves that nice guys do not always finish last.

So why do I think that anger is the only way to get him to respond to my needs? While Matt may not remember what all of our little fights were about, he will certainly remember how I made him feel. What I'm learning through Matt—and what he's learned through his work as a lawyer—is that an argument can be constructive or destructive, productive or unproductive. Your words can be helpful or hurtful. Accusations and moralistic judgments don't help the situation. It's a fallacy to think you can say whatever you please to your spouse. You can't take back hurtful words. So why do I sometimes forget the importance of good manners in marriage?

I try to remind myself that Matt is only human. He wasn't trying to be spiteful. Like all of us, he has his flaws and makes mistakes, but he never intends to hurt me. I know that he wants to do what is right and fair. But sometimes it's hard to trust that he wants what is best for me, although I know that I should.

What I'm starting to realize is that when people say that

marriage is a lot of work, what they mean is that it's a lot of self work. You can't keep your feelings frozen inside you and expect to be loved. Nor can you mask your emotions with anger. When it's hardest—when you're hurt—is the time you need to open up the most, letting go of your verbal defenses. Nobody who takes all of those punches will be left standing in the end. There has to be a better forum for conflict than a boxing ring, which leaves people dazed and confused. It's time we hang up our boxing gloves. And so I squeeze his hand once, my way of apologizing. I hope he understands.

TWENTY-EIGHT

What about Privacy?

Let the past drift away with the water.
–Japanese Proverb

*G*et out!" I yell at Matt, and almost break the bathroom door by slamming it shut in his face. I know he's standing on the other side of it feeling hurt, but I don't care. I've warned him several times to knock first, knowing that one of these days, he's going to catch me in a compromising position.

Thirty seconds later, as I'm combing out my wet, tangled hair in front of the mirror, I hear him knock. "The good news is that my nose isn't broken," he says through the door, and I laugh and open it for him. But I use my body to block his entrance.

"You can come in now because you knocked," I say pointedly, and he grins, tugging at the towel my wet body is wrapped in. But I pull away from him and swat his hand. "Never open the door while I'm in here unless I give you permission."

"Dear, we're married," he says and lovingly squeezes me. I shake my head at him, glancing at his mirrored reflection, his face lightly freckled from the summer sun.

"When I'm in the bathroom, I need my space," I say because I don't want Matt to see me rub night cream on my face, floss my dinner's remains out of my teeth, or gurgle mouthwash until it bubbles down my chin. I feel raw and exposed, inelegant and unfeminine. He can wait for the perfumed, made-up person, into which I transform myself, to emerge. Matt, to my dismay, doesn't need bathroom privacy. He'll leave the door open while he's shaving or combing his hair or worse. And so I'll pull it shut for him. I don't need to see him raw and exposed either. Even in marriage, you need boundaries.

But the bigger issue for us concerning privacy isn't about physical space; it's about personal space. It's the difference between the past and the present. When Matt and I moved into our house, we brought with us relics from the past—pictures, letters, report cards, diplomas—all of which we left boxed up in our storage room. And now my curiosity is getting the best of me. Already, I've accidentally found a few pictures of his ex-girlfriends. While I know that they are not my competition, I can't help feeling a little jealous of them since he kept their photos. With every new detail I unearth, I grow more curious. What else is there to uncover? Why is he keeping this stuff?

I'm not a snoop by nature. I believe in privacy. Even as a child, I left my sisters' diaries untouched in their drawers. But, in marriage, do you have free access to your spouse's past?

Meanwhile, Anne is finding that Pete's past is catching up with her. Apparently, his ex-fiancée—Rebecca—signed or engraved every gift that she gave Pete: books, *forever*; a St. Christopher's necklace, *with love*. And now, whenever Anne touches anything of Pete's, she is instantly reminded of his ex. "It's like she peed on everything in our house!" she says with disgust, her nose wrinkling. And while Anne doesn't feel threatened by

Rebecca, she doesn't like that Pete's past continuously intrudes on their present life together.

One day, as Matt and I are cleaning out a closet, I turn to find him paging through an old photo album of mine. It contains pictures of friends and family spanning several years—college, graduate school, as well as my first few years in Minnesota. Suddenly, he shuts it, looking uncomfortable. And then I remember there are other pictures in it as well.

Before I moved into our house, I threw out most reminders of my ex-boyfriends, like pictures and love letters. Gifts from them, like stuffed animals, I gave to Goodwill. This was my way of starting our marriage with a clean slate. But, admittedly, I did keep a few pictures of ex-boyfriends, which now Matt has found.

I didn't keep them because I felt any attachment to the people in them; they were little more than faces staring back at me now. I kept them because they represented slices of my life. And the lessons that I learned during those relationships, both good and bad, hurtful and joyful, are what make me a better spouse for Matt today. But still, I can't help obsessing over what Matt has unearthed in my past. Exactly which pictures did he see? And what did he think of them?

Then I realize that there are parts of myself that I unintentionally withhold from Matt. I haven't reconciled or accepted everything about who I am or mistakes I made in my past. I still have some scars, insecurities, and vulnerabilities that I need to protect. And, just as I can't change my past, nor can I change his. So I decide that whatever he has carefully put away I will leave alone and trust that he'll do the same. We both need our privacy when it comes to our pasts.

TWENTY-NINE

A Calming Effect

A person's fate is their own temper.
–Benjamin Disraeli

On one particularly cold night, I pull into the Lifetime Athletic Club parking lot and step out of my car into the winter wind. This is a typical Minnesota January: it's so cold that you think your bones will freeze before you can make it indoors. The wind licks my face like a cold tongue against an ice-cream cone. Standing there I press the lock button on my electronic clicker, but my car doesn't beep back at me as it usually does. I press the button again. Nothing.

I try to lock the doors manually, but my key doesn't work in the front or rear doors. I try my key in the trunk, but it doesn't fit there either. I grow livid, realizing I've been cheated. What kind of salesperson sells you a used car with keys that don't work?

On my drive home, I think about how differently Matt would have approached buying my car, which I bought before we were married. Matt shops coolly and thoroughly. He would have sat in every comparable car from here to Missouri to make sure that he got the best deal. And he would have pushed every button in it, not only to make sure that everything worked but also to understand all of its features. I shop impatiently and impulsively, willing to spend a few extra dollars to avoid haggling. All I wanted was a compact car that was practical and reliable, without any upgrades for which I'd have to pay more. Easily manipulated by smooth-talking salespersons—I don't perform well under pressure—I turned to the Internet for a no-hassle, no-haggle approach to buying a car. My local bank, whom I trusted, sold used cars with a warranty program online. Through them, I bought a two-year-old Nissan Altima, taking it for a quick test drive with one of their dealers before signing the purchase agreement.

Until now, I've been satisfied with my purchase. But you can't convince me that their mechanics didn't test the keys in each lock. They suckered me, and my warranty on my car has expired. Driving home, I'm comforted to know that I can depend on Matt to help me battle my local bank. He always knows how to fix a bad situation to get me out of trouble, to set my world right and fair again. Just thinking of how I'll return to the dealer with my smart, aggressive lawyer of a husband at my side has a calming effect on me. I can envision it: within minutes, Matt, who can outmaneuver anyone verbally, will have the salesperson jumping, as he protects me with his aggressive nature, glancing over at me with loving concern. If the problem isn't resolved quickly and completely, Matt will insist on speaking directly to the manager, who will rectify the situation.

When I arrive home, I find Matt sitting on the couch watching a Timberwolves game. I toss my keys onto the couch next to him and tell him what happened. He listens, looking from me to the game, and then asks, "Why didn't you check the key in the locks before you bought the car?"

That is the other thing about Matt. While he can easily fix a bad situation, often he can't understand why you got into it in the first place. And he's not one for sympathy. In my shoes, he would have blamed himself for not testing the keys in each lock. But I refuse to blame myself. I am the victim here. It was they who cheated me, not vice versa. "This is the first used car I've ever bought," I say defensively. "I assumed that the keys would work in the door."

"You should have tested them before you bought the car," he calmly responds, and my head starts buzzing like a beehive. Matt likes to restate the obvious. If I spill coffee while pouring it, he'll remind me to be careful when I go to refill my mug.

"Why do you have to do this?" I yell. "Why can't you just listen?" Sometimes, Matt can bring out the worst in me. I want my feelings acknowledged, his sympathies spoken in a language I understand, similar to the one in which I issued my original complaint. I wanted him to be as indignant as I was concerning the bank's dishonesty. But Matt wants to fix things, to solve problems to make sure they don't happen again. And he doesn't know what to do with my vague, emotional answers. He deals better with facts.

"I don't understand why you get so angry with me," he says, his face revealing his hurt. But I don't care. I walk out of the room.

In our bedroom, I wonder how other wives remain calm during stressful situations. Do they find it difficult to hold on to their tongues? Sometimes, when I'm upset or under pressure, I let my emotions take over my thinking, which causes poor judgment on my part in what I say and do. And then I can't think clearly enough about the situation to work toward a solution for it, like just now when I snapped at Matt. Through Matt, who always remains calm, I'm slowly learning that emotions like anger or fear do nothing but intensify the situation. You're better off remaining calm and allowing your spouse to express how he or she feels. While you may not be able to change the situation, you can change how you think about it.

Just as Matt has a calming effect on me, so do I have one on him. He finds it difficult to relax and do nothing. At every moment he needs to feel productive. But, through me, he's realizing that it's more important that we spend quality time together than clean our gutters or mow the lawn. He's learning to enjoy his downtime, rather than cramming it full of tasks.

During the next week, we learn that the used car program my local bank initiated years ago has folded. In fact, it's as if it never existed. Over the telephone, we get routed from department to department, but nobody we talk to seems to have heard of it, and, of course, I've tossed most of my documentation. "Let's just pay to have the locks rekeyed," Matt says. It's more profitable for him to focus on work he can bill rather than wasting time tracking down a ghost of a department. And although at first I'm disappointed—they should pay for their mistakes, not us—I'm also relieved to avoid confrontation. So I make an appointment to have my locks rekeyed, and early one morning, in my car, I follow his truck to the repair shop. I fiddle with the radio station. I hate commercials, and impatiently scan for music I like.

Up ahead is our exit. Matt, I notice, has put on his blinker, so I turn mine on, too. But then a car cuts him off, and sails off the edge of the road, which, unfortunately, is built on a hill. In the air it rolls over and over. I think of the human life that may crumple with the car when it lands. I wait for the metal crunch. But with the roar of the traffic and my radio turned loud I hear nothing. The car crashes into the snow and then bounces like a rubber ball. It rolls until a chain-link fence nets it like a big, tired fish, with no air left in its gills. There it remains, upside down, its side door crushed.

Suddenly the car is unnervingly quiet and still. Matt steers his truck onto the embankment and puts on his hazard lights. I park behind him. I watch as he struggles to keep his balance in the knee-deep snow as he descends down the hill with his yellow deerskin gloves on. I follow him, skidding every few steps.

Matt leans into the crushed car. Then he quickly looks up at me. "Go get my cell phone," Matt says to me. I've stopped about twenty yards from him, not knowing whether to approach. "It's in my gym bag in the backseat of my car. Call nine-one-one, and move your car so that the ambulance can park there."

I fight my way back up the snowy hill. Water seeps into my dress shoes and is bitingly cold on my toes. The highway sounds like a racetrack. I call for an ambulance and then move my car. I'm impressed with Matt. For the first time I can see how clearly amazing this inner calm of his is. Whereas my fear paralyzed me, his ability to stay calm under pressure resulted in action.

I stagger back down the hill. I move closer to the car and peer in. There is a young girl in there, probably a high school student, who is dazed and bruised but conscious. She is suspended upside down, trapped by her hair, which is caught in the shattered sunroof. What feels like an eternity passes. Matt, uncertain as to whether she has a neck injury, doesn't want to move her, so he continues to talk to her, calming her.

"Go find out where that ambulance is," Matt says. "And tell those people to move their cars." I trudge back up the hill. I start to think that I want to develop an inner calm like Matt so that I can defuse any stressful situation that arises in life or simply between us. My impulsive car purchase has taught me that you achieve nothing when you try to function with your mind over-run with emotion. And now, watching him with this young girl, I see how much you gain when you can operate well enough to listen and think clearly.

"Excuse me," I say to the bystanders. "Can you please move your cars so that the ambulance can get in?" They do. When I call 911 again, I am told that the ambulance should arrive soon. A few minutes later, I hear its siren wail.

The paramedics cut the girl's hair and help her out of the car. She stands without their support, but she staggers a bit in the snow like a drunken college student. She pushes her dark hair out of her face and smiles.

After completing a police report, Matt comes back up the snowbank, his stride purposeful, and his cheeks tinged red from the cold. We watch the ambulance drive away. Then Matt puts his arm around me and leads me back to my car. "Stick close behind me, okay?" I nod. And that's why I love Matt. Because he is my hero.

THIRTY

Emotional Infidelity

Marriage resembles a pair of shears, so joined that
they cannot be separated; often moving in
opposite directions, yet always punishing anyone
who comes between them.
—Sydney Smith

Christina had a party the other night, and Matt and I met a friend of hers who is an attorney. Right away, I liked her friend. She was cute and smart and witty enough to tell a good story, which she interspersed with one-liners that kept us laughing. She was warm and kind and asked engaging questions. She was the sort of person with whom I'd like to be friends. But I couldn't help but notice that she was also the type of person who Matt would have been interested in before he met me.

I always know when Matt is attracted to somebody because he gets a little more energetic and complimentary, like he is now. And when he says, "We should set her up with Steve," referring to a friend of his who he lives through vicariously, I'm certain I'm right. Most of the time, Matt's attractions don't bother me, as they're natural, and I have my own. Flirtations can make you feel attractive and alive. And, as he talks to her, he keeps one arm around me and brings me into the conversation, mentioning the little things he adores in me.

But before the night is over, they exchange business cards and mention having lunch. This is common in Matt's industry. Lawyers who work in firms, like Matt, are always trying to develop relationships with in-house lawyers, like her, who can potentially refer business. As Matt becomes more senior in his firm, it becomes increasingly important for him to bring in new business, to be an originator. While I know that this is the perfect opportunity for him to develop a new and potentially profitable business relationship, I can sense a chemistry here that makes my stomach a bit uneasy. She has a particular combination of traits that worry me: first, she's athletic and attractive, both of which would make her appealing to Matt. Plus she also has the same job as Matt does—the same goals, pressures, and deadlines—which means she'd understand his aspirations and frustrations in a way that I don't.

We leave the party shortly after eleven o'clock. As we merge onto the highway, I ask Matt not to have lunch with her.

"Why not?" he asks. It's hard to go from here, to tell Matt what I am feeling. I trust Matt, I really do. Those jealousies and insecurities I experienced early on in our marriage, those born out of fear and possessiveness, are waning. I know that a harmless flirtation or even a light crush poses no threat to what we have. But I also am aware of how easily affairs can spring up in the workplace, how what starts out as a platonic friendship can escalate to risky business.

"I'm just not comfortable with it," I say.

"Why not? I'll bring another attorney with me if it makes you more comfortable," he says, "I think she could refer some good business to us."

"I know," I say. "And I'm sorry, but I'm just not comfortable with you meeting her for lunch."

"I love you," Matt says. "You know I would never do anything to jeopardize our marriage." And while I believe him, I also think that you should set behaviors that protect your marriage.

Matt laughs at the concept of emotional infidelity. He thinks either you're cheating or you aren't. And while we both agree that physical acts, like kissing or holding hands or more, are cheating, we disagree about that gray area, where you say you're "just friends," but are you really? So what is emotional infidelity, and why does it matter?

At two different companies for which I've worked I've seen affairs spring up, innocently enough, I've imagined: a working lunch, a happy hour, a business trip. Opportunities for infidelity abound in the workforce. And often they start as a friendship. You share your personal feelings about life and your spouse, because it's easier to share what you're feeling with your friend than to risk sharing it with your spouse. Maybe it's a complaint about your relationship or your job, a complaint that you don't share with your wife or husband, and so, over time, you become less intimate with your spouse and more intimate with your friend. Or perhaps you flirt with your friend for that rush, that temporary high, and the person with whom you live day to day dulls in comparison. Soon you become emotionally invested in your friend, who eventually morphs into your office spouse. And then it's only a matter of time before your intimacy at home and your intimacy in the office become confused.

So I want to make sure that Matt and I are doing whatever we can to protect our marriage. It's not that I don't want Matt to have female friends. I just want him to be careful of friendships he makes outside of our marriage, to be careful of friendships that replace or mimic our intimacy. He shouldn't find himself confiding in his friend before he does me.

But how exactly do you protect your marriage from emotional infidelity? My rule used to be simple—don't do what you wouldn't do in front of your spouse. But that rule may be over-simplified. There are little things we do to remind ourselves that our marriage comes first: we keep photos of each other on our desks and attend one another's work functions. But relationships develop over time, not in one moment or one lunch. And so on our drive home I ask Matt to watch for the routines, the patterns he may develop with friends—like stopping by their office each morning for a chat, breaking for coffee at ten or lunch every Thursday. I ask him to be mindful of how intimate and personal his conversations with other women get.

"Dear, if it's important to you, then I will be careful," he says, as he reaches over and squeezes my knee. And then he says he won't go to lunch with Christina's friend, either. I feel silly, a little ridiculous to make such a request, but I'm satisfied by his response.

THIRTY-ONE

You're My Family Now

*Unless you can find some sort of loyalty, you cannot
find unity and peace in your active living.*
–Josiah Royce

For the third weekend in a row, a family member of Matt's is staying with us. I'm ready to hide in the basement. Whenever they visit with all of their children, our home, which is usually quiet, feels like Chuck E. Cheese's. I didn't grow up with this amount of traffic in my home, and I find it unnerving. Matt, however, likes the noise. As a child he watched as his parents welcomed all sorts of overnight guests into their home. Cousins and foster children permanently resided with them. And today, Matt embraces their philosophy of having a home open at all times to friends and family. But, for me, a home is a place of quiet, of refuge. Having frequent houseguests makes me miss my time alone with Matt.

"This has to stop," I say to Matt, because I don't think I can share our home for another weekend. Minneapolis is centrally located for his family, and so they like to stay at our place whenever they're flying out of the airport or driving anywhere else in the Midwest. As his family is enormous, we host a different sibling, aunt, uncle, cousin, or parent at least one weekend each month. Our record is six weekends in a row.

"But I like when my family visits," he says. He loves the familiarity he has with them, the sharing of traditions and the past.

Matt doesn't understand in-law stress, as my family is on the East Coast and hasn't visited us since the wedding. His family's visits are starting to drain me of the energy I need to make our marriage work. And it's more than just the physical energy I use up by cooking, cleaning, and grocery shopping while preparing our home for guests. It's also the emotional energy our houseguests take. Matt works long hours, so I spend more time entertaining his family than he does. That time we have left over at the end of the day to reconnect goes to them, not us. And sometimes when his family visits, he'll take time off from work, which means he'll have to make it up later in the week, and that, too, cuts into our regular time together. What he doesn't understand is that I feel we can't move on in our marriage until we set boundaries with them.

I knew Matt was a different person from me. But what I didn't take into consideration was that meant his family was different from mine. That doesn't mean that I don't like Matt's family. They are wonderful people. I'm touched by the generosity of his sister, Liz; impressed by the intellect of his sister, Ann; endeared by the kindness of his brother, Luke; intrigued by the independent spirit of his sister, Amanda; and charmed by his brother, Walter. But what it does mean is that I will have an adjustment period with them, too. When you marry, you commit to relationships with your spouse's family. It's not fair to ask Matt to choose me over his family. For his sake, I need to make my relationship with them work.

When his sister, Liz, visited, a dinner for six ballooned into a dinner for thirteen. Matt's idea of entertaining is to ask each guest to bring a dish to share, like a salad or bread or dessert. My idea of entertaining is to host, to provide our guests with a nice meal that took a few hours to prepare, complete with a glass of wine, red or white, depending on what's served. But, with my limited skill, there was no way that I could cook a gourmet meal for thirteen people. So I put away my Williams-Sonoma cookbooks and the tools I needed for their recipes. We hauled up an old wood table from the basement and set it beside our glass dining room table. We put out mismatched plates, some of which are chipped, because we only have eight place settings. And the food was no longer about quality; it was about quantity. One sister cooked a ham while another whipped up a carrot soufflé. And, as I stood there mashing garlic potatoes, I realized that there went the elegant dinner I had planned, with its perfectly folded napkins and crystal stemware. It was buffet time.

Meanwhile, Brenda is experiencing her own adjustment period in her marriage, too. She had underestimated the pressure of being both a newlywed and a stepmother. While Mike's first marriage may have ended, his relationship with his ex-wife never will because of their six-year-old daughter. And Brenda, who's not used to parenting, is unsure of what her role should be in her stepdaughter's life. Unaccustomed to her "instant family," she confides that at times she feels like an outsider in her own marriage. When Mike and his daughter bike to the park, she stays home. "I'd rather be alone than feel like a third wheel," she says. What she finds challenging is that Mike doesn't expect there to be an adjustment period for her. He assumed she'd fall into her new role as a stepmother naturally. He tells her that she'll never feel as though they're a family if she doesn't spend time with him and his daughter. Lately, she has made an effort to accompany them on their outings. At times, she still feels out of place, but her relationship with Mike's daughter is slowly improving.

As with your spouse, you can't change your in-laws; you can only manage your expectations of them. And I don't want Matt to lose his closeness to his family. While they're good houseguests—they clean the kitchen after they use a dish; they wipe crumbs that fall while they're buttering toast; they unload the dishwasher without asking where each plate or cup or bowl belongs—Matt and I are a family now, and our needs, like uninterrupted time together, must come first. So I decide to ask Matt to limit their visits. I know how hard it will be for him to close his home to them, when he has always prided himself on keeping it open.

"I can't do that," he says. "Who would I ask to stop coming?" Would he ask his sister, who's traveling through Minneapolis on her way to Iowa, to stay at a hotel for a night? Or his brother, who is car shopping in the Twin Cities? And what about his dad, who he hasn't seen in two months?

"I need to feel a sense of control in my home, and I can't do that when we constantly have houseguests," I explain.

"If you'd like them to visit less, then you need to talk to them," Matt says. But it's his family, not mine, and they will be more receptive to interference run by him than by me.

"You're my family now, and you need to support my needs!" I say. I don't want this to be my problem; I want this to be our problem. We need to provide a unified front so that I don't isolate myself from his family.

"But I'm not the one who has a problem with it," he argues.

So how do you go from being two people to one, with your

loyalties to each other? And how do you let go of your families for each other?

Matt and I do not come up with a solution, although this issue continuously arises. And then, one afternoon while we're all sitting around the kitchen table, Matt's mom asks me how I feel about all of the visitors.

This is a hard conversation for me. I like Matt's mom, and I don't want her to take how I feel about her family's visits personally. But I also realize I cannot be happily married, that I cannot feel at peace in my home, with the constant interruption. It's hard enough trying to sort out who you are in marriage and what you represent. It's even harder to find your identity when you feel constantly outnumbered. But if Matt's family doesn't know that something bothers me, they can't deal with it. And so I tell her how I feel.

"You have to put on your own oxygen mask before you can help anybody else," she says to me, respecting how I feel. "And Matt, if you don't spend time alone with Jennifer and listen to her needs, your marriage will fall apart. She is your family now."

I'm surprised to discover that when I take a risk with Matt's mom, she responds with honesty and integrity. She is sensitive about our relationship and wants it to succeed as much as we do. I don't believe in letting your parents solve your problems; you need to develop the skills within your marriage to work out your problems yourself. But the advice Matt's mom dispenses is invaluable. Matt realizes that in marriage, you must leave your nuclear family to start your new family. And her choice—to give Matt fully to our marriage, rather than keeping him in his role as her son—gives us the glue our relationship needs.

While Matt and I still do not agree on what appropriate

boundaries with in-laws are, his mom has started a dialogue between us. Before Matt says yes to his family's visits, he checks with me. "What do you think, dear?" he asks, which helps me feel more in control. But still, I don't feel comfortable saying no when I know how much he wants to say yes.

THIRTY-TWO

Happy Holidays

To perceive Christmas through its wrapping
becomes more difficult every year.
—E. B. White

On Christmas Eve, Matt and I sit in a Holiday Inn hotel room eating stale nachos and watching a pay-per-view movie. We are stranded in Syracuse, New York, the only airport in New York State to have remained open during this winter storm. Our baggage has been lost by the airline, and the dark winding roads into Ithaca, our final destination, have been closed because of ice, snow, and poor visibility. Our spirits are as mucky as the roads. Matt hates to get stuck while traveling. Wasting time irks him, especially when it's out of his control. Sprawled out on the hotel bed, I sigh, thinking about what a disaster our first Christmas together has become.

We knew that holiday seasons would require compromise. And we were lucky; neither of our families pressured us to follow their routines. They allowed us to decide what would be best for us. Matt and I agreed that for now we'd like to share our holidays with our families, although in years to come we may choose to stay home. Nothing will be set in stone during this first year. Rather, we'll experiment with our different traditions and discover what works for us and what doesn't.

With the distance between our parents' homes, the only fair way to split the holidays was to alternate Thanksgiving and Christmas between them. We felt guilty having to choose one family over another to visit first, but we knew we couldn't make everybody happy at once. We decided on Ithaca for our first Christmas. That way, we'd be on the same schedule as my sister, Christina, who alternates holidays with her husband's family.

Before we left our home in Minneapolis, we tried to make the holiday part ours. What I've always liked about the holidays is that feeling of togetherness, a cozy closure for the year. My mom mastered creating a holiday aura: Cupid left candy on place mats at the kitchen table on Valentine's Day; leprechauns hid sacks of chocolate coins around the house on St. Patrick's Day; and the Easter bunny hid jelly beans on the windowsill, in our dresser drawers, and behind the couch. But with just Matt and me in our half-furnished home, who knew where to start. How do you merge two family traditions to make a holiday yours?

We started with the basics. We bought a tree that met both of our requirements—a live fragrant one that dropped few needles—from the Boy Scouts and propped it up in the living room. On its limbs we hung the eight ornaments we had collected, as well as decorations Matt had made during his childhood from clothespins and bottle caps and yarn. He played the Christmas CDs he had bought at Starbucks, hitting Repeat whenever his favorite song, "The Little Drummer Boy," was on. Our house smelled like pine and cinnamon-scented candles and charred firewood. But still, that Christmas spirit, that magic combination of wonder and hope that we felt at the mall, in restaurants, and at the movie theater, seemed to be lacking in our home.

And now, stranded in this hotel room, I wonder if the Christmas spirit will ever truly arrive for us. Right now, this holiday feels haphazard and confused, with nothing to mark it as ours. It doesn't feel like Christmas without my sister, Cassandra, insisting on a tree with few limbs because she feels sorry for it, or watching my dad sawing it down. It doesn't feel like Christmas without a breakfast of hot cider and pancakes to warm us afterwards. Here, in this hotel room, Christmas Eve will pass like any other day, which depresses me. I had wanted our first Christmas together to be perfect. But now, with our luggage lost by the airline, we'll wake in a hotel room with our teeth crusted over and no toothbrush, my contacts hardened to my eyes, smelling of sweat because we don't have fresh clothes into which we can change. Will the roads be open by morning?

So how can you and your new spouse feel like a family when you can't make a holiday work?

I know that Anne has had her share of holiday stress. Before she left on a business trip, she made a detailed spreadsheet itemizing each Christmas gift they needed to buy, with columns for the name of the person, the name of the gift, where to buy the gift, the estimated cost of the gift, the final cost of the gift, and a check box to show it had been completed. Then she bought gifts for all of the women and girls, which she diligently wrapped. Pete, she thought, would enjoy shopping for the boys, so she left her list on the counter for him, trusting that he'd make the remaining purchases. "I'm off the hook for Christmas shopping," she proudly announced, envisioning Pete running from store to store, crossing items of her list with each gift he wrapped. But when she returned home, she found the list where she had left it.

"We can shop later," he said, but Christmas was only three days away. So there she was rushing from crowded store to crowded store, stuck in endless lines. But now, she's finished her shopping and is looking forward to their first Christmas together. They're spending it alone. Pete's family believes that once you are married, you need to create your own traditions, and so his parents, who live in North Dakota, encouraged him to stay in Minneapolis. Anne, without any family tradition of her own, agreed to try it. And now, with nothing in front of them except for a thawed turkey, martinis, and rental movies, she feels completely at peace. I wish Matt and I had decided to stay home, too.

But here, in the hotel room, Matt is growing restless watching our pay-per-view movie. If a movie doesn't grab his attention in the first fifteen minutes, then he doesn't have the patience to wait to see if it will. He wiggles his feet. He taps the remote control against the nightstand. I can't enjoy a movie when I know that the person I am with doesn't like it.

"What else can we do?" I say. "We're trapped, stuck. We should have stayed in Minneapolis." How do you make the best of a situation when there's nothing, not even a change of clothes, with which to make the best of it?

But, for Matt, ignoring a problem is never a solution. His theory is why focus on what is wrong when the only thing you can do is make it right? He won't wait for some external force to make Christmas Eve special for us. "I'll be right back," he says, and leaves our room. I turn off the television, bored by the movie, too.

Fifteen minutes later, there is a knock at the door. Somehow Matt has managed to scrounge up two beers, which he dangles in front of me. "Put on your bathing suit," he says, and laughs, because neither of us knows where our suitcase is. But together, we go downstairs to sit by the hot tub that is next to the pool. Matt grins at me. We roll up our pants and drop our legs into the water, the warm water bubbling up around us. Underwater I rest my feet on his. He splashes me, and I laugh, relieved to smell a little like chlorine now instead of just sweat. I'm surprised to find how much I am enjoying myself. Maybe we'll never have the perfect Hallmark card holiday, but what does it matter? What we do have is each other, and what's important is that we're together. And that is good enough for me. Little things like mistletoe, wreaths, and gifts don't make the holiday; we do.

Early the next morning, we start our drive to Ithaca in high spirits. Most of the roads have been plowed and salted, with snowbanks so high they're like highway retaining walls. We arrive midmorning to find my family seated around the tree waiting to open their gifts. And the frenzy begins.

THIRTY-THREE

Great Expectations

Life is so constructed that the event does not,
cannot, will not match the expectations.
—Charlotte Brontë

I open our front door to find a UPS man in a brown uniform holding a package and a clipboard. I hope the package is for me. I love unexpected gifts like the ones my mom sends me—books, socks, candy, and anything else she thinks I may need. "I have a delivery," he says. "Would you please sign for it here?"

Of course I will sign for it. I can't remember what I ordered—perhaps it's a late wedding gift? I take my package inside and I open it. Packaged in bubble wrap I find two cell phones, one for Matt and one for me, and, once again, I curse our telephone company.

For the past three months, I've opened our telephone bills to find charges for services we didn't order, like three-way calling and call forwarding. As soon as our telephone company removes one charge, another one seems to appear on our bill. And so once again—for the third month in a row—I find myself on the phone with a customer service representative who is absolutely impossible.

"If you signed for the cell phones, then you must pay the cancellation charges," she says. All of the fine print came inside the box, not outside of it.

"But I never asked for them!" I sputter.

"You signed for them," she repeats. I argue my point with her, my throat catching. She mechanically reiterates her company's policy. I hang up, frustrated and powerless.

When Matt returns home from work, I show Matt the cell phones still in their bubble wrap. "Can you please call our phone company tomorrow and take care of this?" I ask him.

"I can't. I'm swamped at work tomorrow," he says. "Besides, you know the history of all of the problems we've had with the phone company. So don't you think you're the one who's better equipped to deal with this problem?"

I don't respond at first. For three months, I've been waiting for Matt to step in, to deal with the situation swiftly and effectively, calmly and authoritatively. He knows how much I hate conflict. But he refuses to fight little battles for me, expecting me to be self-sufficient and resilient.

"You don't care about me," I say to Matt, because he won't call the telephone company. And I don't say this to be manipulative; I say it because it is how I feel. If he loved me, wouldn't he do this for me when he knows how uncomfortable conflict makes me? Aren't husbands supposed to *want* to protect their wives?

Matt hates when I feel sorry for myself. "It's a telephone call," he says. "You can handle it. What you need to do is know what you want from them before you call, and then ask for it. Stay calm. When you get angry, you lose."

Now I'm completely frustrated. How difficult would it be for him to make one simple phone call? He's a more convincing talker than I am. What takes me three or more phone calls to accomplish he does in one.

Matt is not the rescuing prince, the knight in shining armor, I thought my husband would be. While he's handsome and smart, athletic and witty—all of which attracts me to him—he's not interested in becoming my caretaker. And I admit that I have a touch, perhaps more than a touch, of the victim syndrome. There's something about being taken care of that makes me feel feminine. I thought as a husband Matt'd enjoy a role as a caretaker, that when our newly installed blinds broke, he'd call for the repairs; that when the garbage needed to be taken out, he'd haul the dirty bags to the curb; that when bills needed to be paid, he'd write the checks and balance our accounts. Yet instead of a husband who shows his love for me by killing spiders, I have one who'd like it if I'd crawl under the car with him to change the oil. What I'm discovering is that marriage doesn't excuse you from having to do all of those things you did before.

I find myself growing increasingly frustrated that Matt has no desire to run interference between me and the world. And so I wonder, does any bride find her prince in marriage? Or am I just one of the unlucky ones who found a prince, only not the right one for her? And what do you do when your husband refuses to be who you want him to be?

The next morning, as I drive to the bookstore, I think to myself, *I'm a reasonably intelligent person, and so is Matt. Together we can fix this disconnect between who he is and who I want him to be. All we need is a little bit of self-help, the kind that comes in ten simple steps.* As I stand there pulling book after book from the shelf, I find just the thing: the Oprah-endorsed

Dr. Phil. I like his quick solutions and snappy phrases, which are easy to memorize, like that jingle you can't get out of your head after watching a commercial. They give me a directive; they give me a plan. And sometimes, during arguments, they give me a retort. "Get real," I say to Matt, when I feel he's seeing a problem only from his perspective. During the day, I e-mail Matt advice that I find on Dr. Phil's Web site, highlighting the portions that I think apply to him. Admittedly, advice that works in theory is often difficult to put into practice. It's hard to change the patterns and behaviors you've set throughout your life. But still, knowing that a solution does exist makes our problems feel manageable.

Matt grows tired of me constantly trying to fix our relationship. "Dear, do not quote Dr. Phil again," he says. "Not even in e-mails." If you constantly dwell on the negatives in your marriage, will that be all that you see? Will you contaminate your relationship with that sort of negative energy?

I wonder if I'm making our marriage more difficult than it needs to be. Our relationship will never be perfect. Sometimes it's difficult to remember that Matt is not me. He doesn't think the way I do and won't always express his love the way I want him to. For all of the problems I think we have, maybe only one thing is wrong—our expectations of each other and what marriage should be. So maybe happiness is all about perspective. You can't change your spouse; you can only adjust your expectations, although learning to accept them for who they are can be difficult to do. But you can't depend on your spouse for your happiness.

By forcing me to be self-reliant, Matt is helping me grow into a stronger person, rather than crippling me as an enabler would. And I know that my life isn't perfect. I'm not perfect. There are personal and professional relationships that I struggle with, for which I wish I could find solutions, impasses I wish I could resolve, and gaps I wish I could close. Slowly Matt is giving me the strength to deal with them, to trust myself to do what is right and to forgive myself for past failures.

So I take a deep breath and call the phone company.

"I don't want the cell phones," I said. "I am returning them to you. I do not want to be charged for them."

"Ma'am, you signed for the cell phones," she said.

"This isn't negotiable," I said. "I'm mailing you back the cell phones today. Do not charge me for them." And it worked. I took the phones to the post office that day and never heard from the phone company about the cell phones again.

THIRTY-FOUR

Let's Cuddle

One half of the world cannot understand the
pleasures of the other.
—Jane Austen

Breathing space, my dear," Matt says, groggy-eyed, as he lifts his head up off his pillow. I sigh and roll back over. I'm guilty of three charges: breathing on his neck, pinning him down with my legs, and pressing my bare feet against his. Matt says that at night my body is like a furnace. It heats his up until he feels as if he's suffocating on a bed of hot coals. Sometimes, he puts a pillow between us to stop the heat generation.

"I never get to touch you," I complain. It's early in the morning, and due to our open window I can hear the birds chirping outside. Matt, I'm sure, wishes to sleep a little longer. He has a stressful day ahead of him. But, right now, I need that feeling of connectedness that his physical affection provides. I'm addicted to Matt's muscular body, to the warmth it provides, and to the touch of his hands, firm and solid on my body. But what I'm finding is that our different schedules and internal body clocks are robbing us of our physical intimacy.

At the end of a hard day, Matt craves his personal space. He'll embrace and kiss me shortly after he walks through the front door, but that's it. He'll wander back to our bedroom to remove his suit and tie and silky socks, emerging for dinner wearing a T-shirt and shorts, his feet bare. We'll talk about our day, gossip a little, even, as we enjoy our dinner. Sometimes we splurge on a bottle of wine or dessert. After dinner, after we've stored all of our leftovers in airtight Tupperware containers, he'll go through his nightly routine of opening his mail, flipping through whatever magazine arrived that day, and listening to his phone messages, while I'll sit down to write. At ten p.m., we'll meet downstairs in our family room, where we watch the local news. He looks so inviting sitting on the couch, so I'll pester him for another embrace or to cuddle. But he'll perform what I've come to refer to as the full body block, where he crosses his arms over his chest with his elbows pointed out so I can't approach.

Without looking at a clock, I know from how my body slows that ten-thirty p.m. has arrived. I'll try to coax Matt upstairs with me, but he doesn't like to lie down until he is ready to retire for the night, as he falls asleep. And so, downstairs in our family room, we'll kiss each other good night, a quick parting peck. Some nights he works in the office for an hour or two after the news. On other nights, especially during the NBA season, I can hear him switch the television station over to ESPN. Matt loves *SportsCenter*'s nightly recaps. In our bedroom, I'll pull the comforter over my shoulders, wishing he'd join me for some cuddle time. It's here alone in bed that I feel a lack of physical intimacy between us. For me, physical intimacy requires a special sort of touch—the difference between a grope and a loving caress, a grab and a warm embrace—plus it has an emotional component, like that pillow talk that ties you together at the end of the day. And I can't understand why Matt doesn't crave that emotional component, that honest and selfless sharing of what's in your hearts, as much as I do.

And then, an hour or two later, Matt'll come upstairs ready to frolic. For him, physical intimacy means sex, the quickest and most direct route. But I'll refuse to wake up. "Don't touch me," I'll say, pushing his hands off me, and then feel badly for it. It's not fair for only one of us to control when and how our intimate moments happen. I know how important it is to keep your sexuality at the forefront of your marriage. But still, at that hour I'm too tired to participate. Why do we always seem to have opposite needs at opposite times? Do other wives find their bodies on different timetables than their spouses? If so, how do they reconcile their hectic schedules?

In marriage, the bedroom is another arena in which you must compromise. And so, here I am at six a.m., trying to create an opportunity instead of waiting for him to initiate. But, at the moment, he prefers sleep to me touching him. "I need to feel love," I say, pressing one hand against Matt's bare back to wake him, trying to explain why his timing last night didn't work for me. I wonder if he's quietly hoping I'll fall asleep before I complete my thought. Does he secretly wish that I'd stop overanalyzing everything about our relationship? But I can't stop myself. I need him to understand that for me sex is fleeting. While I enjoy the intimacy the act provides, the depth to which it takes our relationship, when it's not paired with its emotional counterpart, I'm left feeling empty, needing more. I need him to actively listen to me, to understand what I am feeling, to stay connected to me throughout the day using simple physical acts that show he cares, like a smile, a hug, or a pat on the back.

He folds my body into his then, if only to get some sleep, but I'm contented to feel his warmth.

THIRTY-FIVE

The Rule Buster: It's Your Family, Not Mine

By three methods we may learn wisdom: First,
by reflection, which is noblest; Second,
by imitation, which is easiest; and third by
experience, which is the bitterest.
—Confucius

On our front porch, Matt and I wave good-bye to his brother, who's backing out of our driveway. I turn to Matt. "Do you think that whenever your family visits, we could set aside an hour each day for just the two of us?" I don't care what we do—walk through the mall, go running, or drive to Starbucks for a cup of coffee and some quiet conversation. I just need some sort of resolution to our never-ending debate about how much time with family is too much time. "I need quality time for us," I say.

"Time with my family is quality time for us," Matt says defensively, and I think I've insulted him, which surprises me. I thought he'd be touched that I wanted more alone time with him. But Matt is sensitive about any comment I make regarding his family.

"It is quality time with them," I say patiently, apologetically. "But it's not quality time for us."

Whereas I view my family as mine, and his family as his, Matt, ever inclusive, sees us all as one unit, family. And of this he constantly reminds me. "They're your family now, too," he says. "That's what happens in marriage."

How do I convince Matt that time with his family is not quality time for us when his in-laws—my family—live hundreds of miles from us? How do other newlyweds make their spouse understand their position when words aren't enough? And then, I have an idea, a plan. A brilliant one.

I call Matt, who is at work. He picks up on the first ring and authoritatively states his name. "Matt, it's me," I say, hunched over the telephone in my cubicle.

"Hello, dear," he says warmly. In one week, we're leaving for his parents' winter home in Tucson, Arizona. They own a comfortable two-bedroom trailer, with a screened-in porch through which a cooling breeze gently blows. And it looks out over the desert with its stubbly, prickly plants, to the mountains, which have been charred from a recent brush fire. Corralled in the backyard are two of his dad's horses, which we can saddle up and ride.

"How would you feel if my dad went to Arizona with us?"

"Um," he says. Truly, this may be the first time I've known Matt to be at a loss of words. "Are you doing this to get back at me?"

I sigh as if hurt. "Of course not," I say and don't feel guilty for it, as my plan for revenge has morphed into so much more. I always enjoy the time that I spend with my dad. Through Matt, I've learned how to make my family a priority. The more I think about it, the more excited I become about sharing our vacation with him—the hikes through the state park, cold lemonade on the screened-in porch, and barbecuing in the evenings.

"Let me talk to my parents," he says, and I know that they will agree. Their household is completely open to anybody at any time—foster kids, cousins, in-laws—some of whom have remained for years. Because of their generosity they have more traffic than the Greyhound bus station.

"How's he going to get there?" Matt asks cautiously. He knows that an airline ticket at this late date would be ridiculously expensive.

I close my eyes. "I thought he could use some of your frequent-flier miles." Silence. I know how fond Matt is of his hard-earned frequent-flier miles. But we've easily spent their dollar value on groceries, tickets, and dinners for his family. "He's your family, too," I add, knowing that Matt does not like to be hypocritical. He sighs.

After speaking to his parents, Matt agrees that my dad should accompany us to Tucson. But, by the time I call the airline, no seats remain in coach. My dad will have to rule bust at twice as many frequent-flier miles to get a seat in first class.

So I call Matt back. "He needs to rule bust into first class," I say cautiously.

"Um." Matt's sweet side battles his logical one. Then, "Do you really want to do this?"

"I do," I say. I really do. He pauses. And then he agrees.

I book my dad on a last-flight-out, first-flight-in ticket, which counts as one ticket. That means he'll fly into Minneapolis, where coincidentally his connection is, on the last flight out of New York and then, in the morning, take the first flight out to Tucson, which also happens to be our flight. We'll all arrive in Arizona and return from Arizona together.

So there we are on the airplane: my dad in first class, enjoying his hot meal of chicken and pasta, with chocolate cake for dessert, while Matt and I are crammed in economy, eating salted peanuts from a little bag. Matt's legs are jammed up against the reclined seat in front of him, beneath which half of his tray disappears. There's barely enough room for him to work on his laptop, its keyboard pushing into his stomach. But he's kind enough not to mention it.

In Tucson, my dad and I will share the small guest room in which there are two twin beds, while Matt will be relegated to the horse trailer his dad built, where he'll sleep in a bunk. For a bathroom he has the option of the great outdoors or to come inside and use ours. As soon as we arrive at Matt's parents' place, my dad wants to hang up his shirts and pants. "Don't you want to hang yours up, too?" he asks, although he knows that I don't and that I won't. I'll live out of my suitcase, wrinkles and all. But my dad is fussy like Matt. He carefully lines up his toothbrush, razor, and toothpaste in the bathroom, which we will share. He folds his socks after he takes them off at night and tucks them into his shoes. A lifetime with my dad is what has given me the patience and skill for somebody as picky as Matt. My mom credits his neatness to his two-year stint in the army. For years he tried to convert me from my messy habits to his hangers-a-thumb's-distance-apart, bounce-a-quarter-off-the-bed ways. But finally he gave up; I was destined to live in chaos. Soon his only rule when I was growing up was that before I went to bed at night I had to make a fire escape path through my clothes, toys, and books that lay strewn on my bedroom floor.

After we unpack, my dad wants to go to the grocery store to buy bottled water because he doesn't trust the tap water; Matt wants to go horseback riding, but out of respect defers to my dad. My dad wants to take the half-mile flat desert trail a block down the road; Matt wants to hike one of the mountains in the state park, but out of respect defers to my dad. My dad wants to watch the nightly news; Matt wants to sit in the high-backed chairs in the living room and talk, but out of respect defers to my dad. My dad and Matt are similar in that neither likes to deviate from his routine. They both wake up with an idea of what they want to do that day. Matt, who always encourages me to speak up, is learning how difficult it is when you're outnumbered and struggling for acceptance.

Likewise, I'm beginning to understand how challenging trying to please both your spouse and your family can be in your dual role as wife and daughter. But, at the same time, I've never enjoyed a family vacation more than this one. Having somebody there who is firmly connected to my past makes me feel grounded and secure.

Five days later, we fly back to Minneapolis. The next morning, we drive to the airport to see my dad off. As Matt hands his luggage to the attendant, I hug my dad good-bye. "Come back soon," I say, and he promises he will. He shakes Matt's hand.

Together, Matt and I watch my dad clear security, emptying the contents of his pockets into a small dish, waving at him before he disappears into the airport. While walking back to the car, Matt turns to me and begrudgingly says, "It's not quality time for us when family is around, is it?"

THIRTY-SIX

Who Are You?

If two people who love each other let a single
moment come between them, it will grow and it will
become a month, a year, a century
until it becomes too late.
−Jean Giraudoux

Matt and I enter Brit's Pub in downtown Minneapolis to a chorus of, "Congratulations, Matt!" He waves at his legal team who is there to celebrate their trial victory. Then he sees an attorney who he knows ordering a drink at the bar, so he lets go of my hand and walks over to him. I hate being left at the door upon arrival, especially at his work functions.

I walk over to the paralegals who are seated by the window. We're beyond the point of small talk, but not by much. I feel as if I slow down their conversation with all of my questions. I don't understand what they're talking about, or why it's so important. They speak in legalese about experts, briefs, and depositions. After six months of marriage, I still mix up patents and trademarks and copyrights, and have yet to figure out what trade dress means. It's always awkward when you join people who share a close bond from working together. But to feel a part of Matt's life, I try for conversation with his colleagues, and they try for conversation with me. Sometimes it works; sometimes it doesn't. Tonight it's sort of working, as I'm starting to get to know them better. But my eyes trail Matt.

Chris, a paralegal, notices. "He's excited about his victory," she says kindly and motions for me to sit with them. "He wants to share it with people who can appreciate it." She's right; Matt needs an audience that can appreciate his victory, and I'm not it. I didn't realize how important this case was to him. I don't appreciate how much you need to win to be viewed as a successful trial lawyer or how deep that divide is between a victory and a loss. I don't appreciate the millions of dollars that are at stake as Matt fights for his clients' right to sell their product or prevent another company from infringing on their patented invention. And, unlike his colleagues, I don't rise with him at seven a.m. and work until midnight, ordering in pizza while sitting in a conference room-cum-war room, preparing for a cross-examination of a witness.

But Matt didn't share much about the trial when I spoke to him over the telephone at night or about his victory when I picked him up at the airport. I am his wife, so why, at this moment, does he seem like a complete stranger to me? Do other newlyweds ever look at their husbands and wonder, *Who are you?*

Once, I asked Christina if she ever looked at Rob and wondered who he was. "Sometimes," she admitted. Whenever she runs into Rob's old colleagues—he used to work as a music distributor, going backstage at rock concerts, unconcerned with laying down roots of any sort—she feels left out. They easily drop names and histories of bands, half of whom she's never heard of, as she doesn't know much about popular music. She's an NPR gal. "I wonder if we would have hated each other if we had met five years earlier." But, by the time they met, they both had grown and softened, and their life paths seemed more in sync. Still she occasionally wonders if their life trajectories will eventually tear them apart.

And, while house hunting, Anne is experiencing moments where she looks at Pete and wonders who he is, too. In his work as a litigator, he represents contractors who are being sued by individuals whose homes have been damaged due to moisture intrusion, some of whom had to replace all of their siding, which was immensely costly. According to Anne, Pete seems to think every house they look at will eventually fall apart because of water intrusion. And so he crawls around each house with a headband flashlight in search of water that will potentially seep through the siding, the windows, the gutters, the sheathing, or the vapor barrier. This Pete—anal-retentive, detailed-oriented, Construction Pete—is nothing like the Pete she knows.

As Matt and I drive home from the bar, I pout in the car. I'm a master at The Pout. When I'm in a better mood, Matt imitates it by pushing out his bottom lip with his top one, burrowing his eyebrows, and crossing his arms. Now, I hold that position and sigh a little bit to get him to stop concentrating on the road and look over at me.

"What's wrong?" he asks. I don't respond. This is a question to which he should know the answer. I stare out the window, feeling slighted and frustrated, hoping he'll somehow make me feel better. But, without fully understanding how I perceive the situation, how can he offer me any support? Neither of us are mind readers. "Come on, you can tell me," he says. He cups my knee with his hand and shakes it.

"You ignored me all night long," I say.

"I thought you were talking to Chris and Angela."

"Because you left me there!"

"You should have said something," he says. And he's right, I should have. But what would I have said to him? Who are you? And what did you do with my husband?

My anger subsides. "I feel as if there's a part of you I don't know," I say calmly. "It comes out whenever we're with your work people." It's true; I feel there is so much of his life that I am not a part of, so much of it that I don't understand. And it saddens me that there is a part of him that I may never know.

"You know everything."

"I don't know what you do all day long. And I don't know who you are at work."

"Of course you know what I do at work. I work," Matt says. "And you've been to my office before. You've met everybody there."

I've seen his thirty-third-floor office, the cafeteria overlooking downtown Minneapolis, and the refrigerator from which cans of pop and water are freely available. But I've completely lost touch with what his professional goals and achievements are, and I don't want us to drift apart.

So how do you stay in touch with one another? Perhaps I need to pay closer attention to Matt's needs, not just my own. In his own way, he had hinted at how important this case was for him—his stress level, the hours he spent preparing for it, both in the office and at home, turning down social events he would have enjoyed. I should have tuned in to what he was feeling. But I didn't pick up on the significance of what he revealed, nor did I pursue

the subject with him. In the future, I plan to ask Matt more questions about his work, to remember what it is that weighs on him
from day to day. Maybe next time he'll want to share his victory
with me first.

THIRTY-SEVEN

The Bachelor Party

Never does the human soul appear so strong
as when it foregoes revenge, and dares
forgive an injury.
−E. H. Chapin

*J*ohn's getting married," Matt announces when he comes home from work. I clap my hands together, excited for him. I've only met John once. He flew in from Houston, where he lives, to Minneapolis to spend the Fourth of July with us. He was Matt's roommate during "the good old days," when they lived in a dump, fed their dog cornflakes, and referred to each other as wingmen, sharing an irrational optimism in their ability to attract women.

I sigh with relief whenever another one of Matt's bachelor friends stops living what they call the good life—beers, girls, and late-night crawls. Knowing they're settling down makes this life I lead with Matt feel more secure, more socially acceptable, the norm. Sometimes I think he and his friends have a pack mentality, without my best interest at heart. Wives help stabilize and calm them. But then, I remember that with weddings come bachelor parties, which means strippers and lap dances and enough alcohol to drown a donkey.

Why are bachelor parties socially acceptable? Do wives who say they have no problem with strip clubs really not care that their man visits one? Where do you draw the line in marriage? And how do you know when it's been crossed?

I looked the other way for Matt's bachelor party. With the momentum of all of his friends, I felt like I couldn't stop it anyway. And so I tried to convince myself that it was nothing more than a rite of passage, a way for him to shed his single, independent lifestyle and embrace all of the commitments married life requires. But when that didn't work, I fretted to my coworker, Bobbie, who's been married for six years, about it. She rolled her eyes. "It's not the bachelor who you have to worry about," she said. "It's the married men. They are the absolute worst." At the time, her words comforted me. But now all I can imagine is Matt with a roll of dollar bills, puffing on a fat cigar, ogling a barely legal bleached blond girl whose cup size is twice mine. My mind has the tendency to make situations worse than they are.

I've never entered a strip club before but have watched enough Lifetime movies to think I know what goes on inside of them. I don't like what I envision. But, at the same time, I don't believe in telling Matt what he can and cannot do. You have to voice your opinion and trust your spouse to respect your feelings. And so I tell Matt what my limits are—no sexual interaction, like lap dances or touching—and leave the decision as to what is appropriate behavior up to him. But then he casually mentions that the bachelor party will be in Cancún, Mexico. Suddenly, I feel very insecure.

I spent one crazy week in Cancún for spring break while in college. There, girls vied for free beer by having water poured over their white T-shirts while the guys drank so much that their eyes shone like glazed donuts. One night, we saw skinny male strippers in purple G-strings, which did nothing for me but turn my stomach like the sight of slugs would. Moral codes and social judgments didn't apply there. On that small strip of beach, nothing mattered but sexuality and beer. Not even sleep. By the end of the week, you weren't even sure what your own values were; all you knew were the thirteen ways you could drink beer from a can and how to get sand out of your bathing suit without taking it off. And so, I do not want Matt to go there.

"In Cancún, there are no strippers, only prostitutes," I say pointedly. It's not that I think he'll hire a prostitute or that he'll cheat or take off with a stripper. What I'm concerned about is that what we consider appropriate behavior won't apply in a different country code.

Matt simply laughs. "Whether you agree with their premise or not, strip clubs are a harmless form of entertainment for men," he says. "It's just what guys do when they get together." While I do agree that for most men strip clubs are less about the girls and more about a boys' night out, I don't like that he spends our shared money to watch half-naked women dance. If it makes me uncomfortable, why does he do it?

"Tradition," he says with a sheepish grin. This is the answer he gives whenever he doesn't have a better one, although he knows I detest it. To me, tradition isn't an argument *for*, it's an argument *against* oppression, ignorance, and domination. Still, that doesn't stop him from trying it.

I won't come out and say that I don't want him to go to the bachelor party. I know how important it is for him to be there to support John, and he'll only resent me if I tell him to stay home. And I married him because I trust him to respect me; I need to remember that. He'd attend John's bachelor party no matter what, regardless of whether they planned to golf, camp, or watch a sporting event. The girls, I try to remind myself, are incidental.

But I can't change how I feel, and, as hard as I try to be mature, sometimes I'm just not. So I decide to torture him for the next three months instead, to try to convince him not to go without actually saying, "I don't want you to go." At night, while he lies in bed sleeping, I curl up against his warm body and think of questions, like little baited traps, that I can ask him when morning comes.

He rises before the sun. After he showers, he lays three ties against his suit to figure out which one matches best. I roll over in bed and casually ask my first question. "Is touching cheating?" I try to look indifferent.

"Who's touching whom? And how are they touching them?" Logically, I know that's his lawyerese. A simple answer of yes would mean that you'd cheat on your spouse by hugging your mom. But I take his hesitation, his need for further definition, as a sign of guilt.

"So you think it's okay to touch other women?" I ask accusatively.

"What?" I get one of those looks that say I'm bordering on insanity. This is probably one of those times where he's thinking, *I have no idea what is going on in her mind, and I'm better off for it.*

The following morning, after he steps from the shower and towels himself off, I meet him in the doorway to ask another question. "What do strippers look like?" I stare at him, but he's focused on his reflection in the bathroom mirror, running a comb through his short hair.

"It depends on where you go," he says and taps the water from his comb into the sink before putting it back in its drawer.

"So you've been to a lot of strip clubs then?" I ask.

He sighs and goes to get dressed.

Finally, the next morning he stops me midsentence, his hand up like a traffic cop. "Stop. I can't listen to another one of your questions. You can ask me any question that you want a week before I leave. But no more questions before then." And that's it; there goes my fun, my self-inflicted pain.

By the time Matt leaves for his bachelor party, I have nothing left to ask him. I don't know how to explain my fear to him; there doesn't seem to be any female equivalent to which I can relate it for him. It saddens me to know that there is a part of him I will never understand. And so I simply kiss him good-bye at the airport and wish him safe travels.

While Matt is out of town, Bobbie takes me shopping to distract me. I feel like such a stereotype with my credit cards and shopping bags. She picks out a bedspread for our guest bedroom and tells me to buy it and I do. Her home is perfect, like a page out of *Country Living*, and I trust her judgment more than I do mine. I buy the bedspread in part to decorate our house, but more to even things out. For every dollar I think Matt'll give a stripper, I plan to spend one for revenge. Soon, we've got more shopping bags than we can carry, and so we stop to readjust, putting smaller bags in larger ones.

"Do you think he's getting a lap dance right now?" I ask Bobbie, suddenly worried, envisioning a stripper's skinny arms wrapped around his neck.

She looks at me. "Jennifer, you can't control him. He's going to do what he's going to do. So why worry about it?"

She makes a good point. You can't control your spouse or his actions. Obsessing over Matt's trip won't change what he will do or stop him from doing what I don't want him to do. But what I do have control over are my retaliatory actions to his trip. How much damage do I want to cause, just for the sake of getting even? I decide I'm done shopping for the day, so I tell Bobbie that I'm tired, and we go home.

When I get home there is a choppy but loving message from him on our answering machine. I'm touched he called from Cancún. I realize that even if he does spend one night looking at naked women, that won't ruin our marriage. We have so much more between us.

Two days later, I pick up Matt at the airport and ask a breezy, "So how was it?" His face is tanned and lightly freckled like his arms and back. His response is light. "We had fun. What did you do all week?" I tell him about girls' night out; he tells me about a fishing expedition they went on. He's still the same man, as committed to our marriage as ever. And I'm surprised that with that knowledge I feel a sense of relief.

THIRTY-EIGHT

In Defense of Lawyers: Sometimes, It's Okay to Lie

Always be a little kinder than necessary.
–Sir James Matthew Barrie

I bought Matt an expensive glass gavel at the Corning Museum of Glass where it glittered in a lit display cabinet. I thought it'd look great in his office on his desk or one of his shelves. When I gave it to him, he removed it from its box, turned it over in his hand, and asked, "What is it?"

"It's art," I said. "I thought it'd be sort of symbolic for you, since you're a lawyer."

"Thank you," he said, although I knew by his countenance that he didn't like it. He set it back into the black foam in which it was packaged and put the lid on the box, which he set aside. Later, he admitted that it wouldn't have been his first choice as a gift. "I like gifts that are functional, that serve a purpose," he said. "What do you do with a glass gavel?" I wanted to hit him over the head with it.

I've heard the jokes about lawyers, more affectionately known as money-grubbing ambulance chasers. But Matt is the most honest man I know. He won't do anything that is unethical, professionally or personally. He makes sure that he is honest both with his clients and their opponents. When he gives his word, it means something—he'll never go back on it, even if he regrets giving it. And while money does partly influence his choice of profession, he also believes in having a purpose in life and working toward the greater good. Ask him about the patent system, and he will proudly announce that the United States Constitution is the basis for it, that it is the cornerstone of an economic system that promotes entrepreneurialism and innovation. I'm surprised he doesn't have an American flag hanging outside his office door.

I believe in the truth when you're asked for it, when a person looks you in the eye and truly wants it. But I also believe in little white lies, what I consider social graces. I don't need to know that you think my good friend is hot or that you don't like my new haircut or that I have morning breath.

White lies, for me, are ethically tricky. They're all about a judgment call. They can't have any evil intent, and your motivation for telling one can't be self-serving. And they can't be outright lies. They're dressed up half-truths, an alternative answer that's less harsh than the truth.

For example, when somebody gives you a gift that you don't like, and says, "I hope you like it," you don't say, "Thanks, but it's really not my style." You find something you do like about it and express your gratitude that way. "Wow, I've never seen such a shiny gavel! Thanks!" And you set it out in plain sight to show your appreciation for it. The gift, when received, isn't about you. It's about the giver and the thought, care, time, and money that went into the gift.

As difficult as it was for me, I had begun to accept Matt's

brutal honesty as a part of who he was. There was something re-freshing in it; you could count on it. I had to admire him for al-ways being true to himself, to his needs and desires. And I started to wonder if I should become more like him. I find it difficult to deliver a hard truth. When I do, I will do so apologet-ically and halfheartedly to avoid causing you pain. But by speak-ing white lies and other sorts of half-truths, do you give up a part of what you really think to gain acceptance?

I grew adept at asking Matt questions so specific that I could somewhat control his answer. I'd artfully phrase them, leaving no room for ambiguity, so that no matter how he responded, his answer wouldn't injure my pride: *"Does my hair look okay?"* became *"Should I run a brush through my hair one more time?"* *"Do I look frumpy?"* became *"Are these clothes cut right for me?"* *"Do you like my cooking?"* became *"Do you like this new recipe?"* That way, regardless of his answer, I could save face by blaming something else—the wind, the outfit, the recipe—rather than myself.

But then I made a critical error. I asked him a direct question, and his truthful response hurt me more than I ever imagined it would.

I am always reluctant to share my personal writing with oth-ers, which troubled Matt. He saw it as a lack of trust on my part. But, as any writer knows, it's easier to expose your body than your soul. And nothing lights up your soul as clearly as your writing. When I proudly announced that I had finished a raw and intimate essay I had spent years working on, Matt asked to read it. "Not yet," I said, because it revealed my innermost, protected thoughts.

"Dear, don't you think it's time you trusted me?" he asked. I hesitated. I drank a glass of wine. I drank another. And then

I shrugged. I went into the office, booted up the computer, and unlocked the password-protected document for him. While he read my essay, I downed another glass out of nervousness and turned on the television. Finally, he emerged from the office.

He didn't say anything at first. He sat down in the leather chair, put his feet up on the footrest, and picked up the remote control. He stared at the colorful images on the television screen while I stared at him. What was he thinking? I knew he didn't like it; otherwise, he would have praised me immediately. And, as much as I knew I shouldn't ask him a question for which I didn't want a truthful answer, I couldn't stop myself. Maybe it was the wine or the tension caused by not knowing what he thought, but I blurted out, "What did you think?"

He turned the television down and faced me. "It was okay," he said, shrugging. He took a sip of soda. "I found it interesting because I know you, but I guess I expected more from it."

He didn't think twice about his answer. He didn't taint his response for my benefit or apologize for any pain that his answer caused. And telling me that my writing was okay was, in fact, not okay with me. I had completely revealed myself to him, and he said that what he saw inside me was okay. Did that mean that I was just okay?

"You know, Matt, sometimes I'm not asking you for the truth. Sometimes I simply want your reassurance," I said and stalked toward our bedroom door. Before I shut it behind me, I threw him a pathetic, hurt look. He smiled at me sympathetically. *That's it,* I thought to myself. *Never again will he read anything that I write.*

Without turning on our lights, I went over to our bed and crawled under our comforter. I needed some time to think. There, in the dark, I asked myself, *Do you want a spouse who is honest or not? Do you want Matt to censor himself for the sake of your feelings?* I had to respect him for giving an answer that was truthful, risking my hurt and disappointment, my anger even. But how could I be married to somebody who thought that my writing was okay when my life goal was to become a writer? I was hurt, embarrassed even. I closed my eyes and rolled over onto my side, eventually sleeping off my hurt.

I know that I will never change Matt, that I will have to accept his honesty as a part of who he is, as difficult as that may be at times. And I don't want Matt to give up his honesty. What I would like him to learn is how to couch the truth in kindness. While Matt may disagree with me, I still believe that white lies are a part of good manners, of allowing your partner to save face.

THIRTY-NINE

Opposites Attract

Only in love are unity and duality not in conflict.
—Rabindranath Tagore

*M*att and I sit on a chairlift in Colorado with our poles across our laps and our skis dangling from our feet. I'm quiet, looking out over the mountains, thinking how romantic riding on this chairlift would be if Matt would just shut up for one moment. He's not talking to me. He's talking to the man who got on the chairlift with us, and you'd think they were life-long friends. I feel completely excluded from their conversation. I try to think of something light and airy to contribute but can't. Have I become dull and uninteresting, invisible even? This should be our time together, our chance to grow closer to one another.

For a month, I had been looking forward to our vacation. We needed a break from the demands of our everyday marital life, an opportunity to reconnect and remember why we fell in love with each other. So when his aunt Patty invited us to stay alone in her Beaver Creek ski-in-ski-out condo for a week, we eagerly accepted her offer. Seven days together with no distractions seemed ideal. I imagined it: riding up the chairlift gazing at each other; removing our gloves to hold hands; warming our fingers and toes in front of a flickering fire. And Matt, with his endless enthusiasm, perfectly outfitted me for the occasion: goggles for days where the snow fell hard and the wind whipped the bitter cold into our faces, sunglasses for the days where the afternoon sun burned the snow into slush, and lined gloves that claimed to be both waterproof and breathed. "Let's get you a new jacket and ski pants, too," he said, but I refused, saying we had spent enough money.

We arrived at the condo late Saturday night. The following morning, Matt, as always, rose with the sun. We drove to town to rent skis and boots and purchase our passes for the slopes. At the ski shop, Matt fussed over me, asking me to try wiggling my toes in my boots. He stuck my poles beneath my armpits to make sure they were of the right height. Then he grabbed ahold of my leg and tried to move it back and forth to make sure my bindings were secure. I laughed at his fastidiousness, tousling his hair as he bent over. He worried about me, a novice skier, way more than I worried about myself.

Once he was satisfied that I was well fitted, we headed back to the condo to make our first runs before the slopes grew crowded with skiers and snowboarders and the occasional snowshoers. Matt held on to me with one hand so that I wouldn't fall before I got onto the chairlift. And before I knew it, there we were on this four-person chairlift with a man I was suddenly envious of, a man who Matt obviously found more interesting—at least at the moment—than he found me.

I knew I was being selfish, after all of the time and energy Matt had spent planning our trip. But what concerns me about us, and what always concerned me, is how different we are in social settings. Matt has such a busy personality that I often feel as if I'm rushing to keep up with him. When the two of us are together, we spend more time working toward a shared goal than we do talking about life. And it's those moments of peace and quiet, like now on this chairlift, that I covet. They're opportunities to grow closer to one another. So I cannot understand why Matt thinks that investing all of this energy into a complete stranger is better than investing it in me. It makes me feel as if we have nothing in common, that we have nothing left to say to each other—or, even worse, that he doesn't think we need to work at our relationship anymore. And I start to feel like his shadow, his marionette, his unfunny sidekick.

Sometimes, I wonder if my friends have better marriages than Matt and I do. I envy how easily Anne and Pete laugh together, how charming they seem to find one another. And I admire how affectionate Mike is with Brenda. He always seems to have a hand cupping her back. Christina and Rob spend more time together than Matt and I do, and I wonder if that means their relationship is more successful than ours. I know you can never truly comprehend what goes on inside another's marriage by looking at it from the outside. Those you think have healthy marriages may not, while those you think have dysfunctional ones may actually have one that works well for those involved in it. A marriage that works for somebody else won't necessarily work for us, so there is no point comparing ourselves to couples who seem better or worse than we do.

When we get off the chairlift, Matt stops to tighten his ski boots. He likes to ride on the chairlift with them loose. "Did you make a friend?" I ask, but he doesn't get the sarcasm in my voice. He adjusts his ear band.

"He was really interesting," Matt says, his eyes trailing him, while I sulk, using my pole to push the snow off the tops of my skis. I'm not good at telling Matt how I feel. When he sees my face, he pokes me in the butt with one of his poles and asks what's wrong.

I swat his pole away. "You put more energy into strangers than you do me," I say.

"Why didn't you say anything?" Matt asks.

"I would have to interrupt you. Or him," I say. Brenda understands how I feel. When Brenda and her husband, Mike, who's also a talker, are together, we can't get a word in. Matt promises that he won't talk to the next person who gets on the chairlift with us, but that doesn't lift my spirits. Why should I have to force him to focus on me?

He kisses me kindly and gently before starting down one of the trails, swishing back and forth, his skis parallel to one another. As I watch him, I wonder, while opposites attract, how similar must you be to stay together happily? While we were dating, we enjoyed how our differences brought out new and improved versions of ourselves. We learned so much from one another. But now that we are married, our differences are causing some of our needs to go unmet. So, in marriage, how do you keep that spark between you that your differences initially caused from turning into an uncontrollable flame?

That evening, Matt and I grab beers from the refrigerator and head for the hot tub on the patio. I love the feel of the cold air on my face and shoulders while water warms the rest of my body. I look over at Matt. "Do you ever worry that we're just too different from each other?" I ask.

He thinks about it for a moment. "I used to," he says. "But I've been really happy married to you."

I don't want to cause a problem where there isn't one, so I stop talking and quietly sip from my beer. I've been happily married to him, too. But what worries me isn't the present but the future. Will our differences eventually tear us apart? Or is our marriage more important than our individual perspectives on life?

I can't rewire Matt. There's no point trying to change him to be more like me. Perhaps I should focus on what we do have in common, like our core values, our moral outlook on life. We value education, prefer spending our weekend nights at a friend's house or a restaurant than watching television. We choose athletic vacations over sunbathing on a beach, and neither of us thinks twice about hopping on an airplane. Neither of us floats through life. We both like to set goals for ourselves, and we support one another in pursuing them.

Maybe our similarities are greater than our differences. Maybe neither of us needs to change to fit together better. I can be more understanding of his need for social interaction if I feel as if I have quality time with him, too. He can talk to me rather than tapping away on his laptop while aboard an airplane or participating in a conference call while driving. Maybe we just need to create enough space in our relationship for both of our personalities. And perhaps our own world will expand having two perspectives in it instead of just our own.

FORTY

My Debt Is Your Debt

Dare to live the life you have dreamed for yourself.
Go forward and make your dreams come true.
—Ralph Waldo Emerson

While at work, I realize that I will turn thirty in one month. And I'm no closer to my professional life goals than I was at twenty-five. I'm further along in my career, with more responsibility and a better paycheck. But I don't feel validated by the work that I do. I feel consumed by it.

I've always dreamt of taking a year off from work to write a book, but I'd never take that risk without savings or health insurance or housing. But, in marriage, I'm starting to feel a sense of urgency in pursuing my dream. Running a household takes more time and energy than I thought it would. If we eventually throw kids into the mix, I may not have another chance to pursue my dream for years to come. And so, that night, over dinner, I tell Matt how I feel.

At first, I feel silly sharing my dream with him. I don't want him to think I'm unhappy with our life together, or that I'll no longer be a contributing member of our household. But for us to build a future together, he needs to know how I view our road ahead. I won't be content working in a cubicle forever. If we revised our spending habits—neither of us wishes to rely on credit cards to make up for the difference between our salaries and our spending habits—I could comfortably quit now. Matt's salary could support both of us and still allow us to save for unforeseen expenses, like car repairs, unemployment, and medical bills.

"And so, I think I should quit my job," I summarize for him. "This could benefit you, too. I'd be home to keep the house clean, pick up your dry cleaning, and let workers in." Quitting my job may alleviate some of our dual career couple tension.

He thinks for a moment. "Right now is not a good time for you to quit," he says. "The bill for the carpet installation and the downstairs couch are due next month. Plus, we have your student loan payments." Matt is practical to a fault. He doesn't see the point of quitting a perfectly good job for what he considers a hobby. Writing, he claims, is not work. Work is what brings in a paycheck or makes your hands blister and you sweat.

"Those remodeling bills aren't mine. They're yours," I say, because the remodeling—at least, to this extent—was his idea. And whenever we pay off one bill—first from our wedding, then from our honeymoon—another expense arises, typically due to a household project or purchase initiated by Matt.

"When we pay off your student loans, you can quit your job," he says. But the expense of our home improvements prevents us from paying off my low-interest student loans. While perhaps that priority makes sense financially, at this rate I don't see how they'll ever get paid off—and therefore how I'll ever be able to quit my job.

So ultimately who is responsible for the debt brought into a marriage? If money becomes a joint responsibility, then does the debt become a joint responsibility, too? Every financial choice we make affects our ability to pay off my loans.

Anne and Pete are saving for their goal of buying a home. They understand my frustration with student loans. She and Pete are struggling to pay off his from law school. When they first married, they had no jobs and twenty-two dollars in their joint checking account. And so they cut pennies wherever they could. To lower their grocery bill, Anne purchased food in bulk at Costco, like jumbo jars of sun-dried tomatoes, olives, pickles, and nuts, which she then refused to let go to waste. She put the sun-dried tomatoes in pancakes, bread, and eggs for a month, until her husband's stomach turned at the sight of them. Anne is a natural-born saver.

And sometimes they disagreed over how to spend the little money that they had. While Pete is typically frugal, like Matt, when he makes a purchase, it's for something big. When Pete wanted to buy the Total Gym, Anne weighed her options: did she want to save their money to reach their goal of getting out of debt quicker, or did she want to support him in his quest for good health? Anne, who is always planning for the future, decided that his health was more important in the long term. And so she encouraged him to purchase the Total Gym.

He brought it home and assembled it in their spare guest room. When he used it that night she was delighted. Night after night she waited for him to use it again, but he never did. After a few weeks, she decided to use it herself, thinking perhaps he'd be inspired by watching her. She exaggeratedly grunted and groaned while lifting and pulling on the weights. She flexed and told him how great her muscles felt after her workout. But her plan didn't work. He never used the machine again. Today just looking at that machine irritates her.

And while that transitional time during which they had no money was difficult for them, Anne is thankful for it. "At first, I didn't know how we'd ever make it," she says. "But now we know that we can overcome any obstacle to make our marriage work." Today both have good jobs and are financially ready to purchase a house.

While I cannot get Matt to agree to let me quit my job, I do get him to commit to stop spending money so that in the future it can become a possibility. But then we discover that our shower is leaking. Matt asks, "Didn't you notice that water from the garage ceiling was dripping on your car windshield?"

"I don't think so. But if I did, maybe I just thought it was raining," I say.

"In the garage?" he asks, lifting his eyebrows just a bit. I blush. I don't always think before I speak.

The plumber delivers worse news. The plywood floor in our bathroom is rotted, which he discovered while walking on it. His boot went through the floor. Fortunately, he wasn't hurt. We'll have to gut the bathroom and lay a new floor and build a new shower, tile by tile. Since our toilet and cabinetry are outdated, he suggests we replace those, too.

Matt meets with an interior design firm. With him in charge, I know our bathroom won't just get redone. Soon it will be the nicest room in our house. And I'm right: he orders real stones for the shower floor and walls, custom-design cherry cabinets with a granite countertop, and crown molding to match. The cost, I know, will be immense. I don't want to know what the final figure will be. I stop asking Matt how much money we are spending, and he stops volunteering it.

One day, shortly after our bathroom remodeling project is finished, I find Matt in his bathroom, staring down at the floor, stepping from stone to stone, his feet bare. "What are you doing?" I ask.

"I'm trying to figure out where they put the floor heat."

"The what?" When I discover that his floor heating system cost us an extra two thousand dollars, just so he can warm his bare feet when he steps from the shower, I'm livid. I've never heard of such a frivolous expense. Floor heat? What ever happened to wearing thick socks?

"Do you have any idea how cold stone can get?" he asks. He adds that his bathroom floor wouldn't retain heat as it's over our garage.

"Stand on your bath mat then," I say. His hunter green Ralph Lauren bath mat had cost us close to a hundred dollars. I'm ready to tape it to the bottom of his feet just to make sure he gets our money's worth out of it.

"But the bath rug only covers a small part of the floor," he says.

"What about a heated toilet seat?" I retort. "Would you like that, too?" If we needed my income to pay our mortgage, utilities, or to support our children, I wouldn't fathom quitting my job. But to keep working just so that we can buy new furniture or a new rug or floor heat, none of which I want nor need, seems senseless to me. And having him put floor heat before my lifelong dream hurts too much.

So I approach the subject of quitting my job with Matt again. I try to impress upon him that I am not materialistic, that I do not get the same sort of pleasure from our home improvements that he does. While he understands this in the abstract, he doesn't understand why I'm not delighted by how wonderfully our house is coming together. "Our house looks great; I'm not denying that. But what's important to me isn't that we buy a new sofa, a new dining room table, or a big-screen television," I say. "What's important to me is that I have a chance to go after my life's dream."

He thinks for a while. He considers my position. "What sort of time line would you have?" he asks. "What is your plan? What are your goals?" I know how difficult it would be for him to think I am sitting home doing nothing while he's at the office. With no milestones to mark my progress, he won't know how to measure it. He wants to know what my expectations are.

To be honest, I don't have a plan, aside from waking each morning to a pot of coffee and spending endless hours writing. I don't know what I will write. While I argue with Matt, saying that he doesn't provide me with a report for his day, so why should I provide him with a report for mine, I do wonder what I would do all day. Would I really be able to write, or would I squander the time?

I take him up on his offer to review where I'm at in my writing career in a few months. That night, we sit down together and list what my goals are. I decide to start working on a book proposal. If I make some progress on it, then we'll reconsider whether I should quit my job.

FORTY-ONE

The Rental Property

What do we live for, if not to make life less difficult
for each other?
—George Eliot

Years ago Matt purchased a small house in a trendy section of town, which he lived in during his bachelor days. With property values in that neighborhood skyrocketing, neither of us wanted to sell it nor did we want to live in it. And so we decided to rent it out. That is, I decided to rent it out. Matt was ambivalent. With his work hours, he didn't have time to manage tenants or schedule services. And so he said that if we kept it, managing it—finding tenants, answering their late-night calls, and meeting repair persons—would have to be my responsibility. I was fine with that. I liked the idea of running my own rental business.

"Are you sure you want to be a landlord?" he asked, surprised. His brow wrinkled.

"What's that supposed to mean?" I asked defensively. I knew what he meant. He didn't think I could do it.

"I don't think you'll like it. You don't like conflict." At garage sales, I'm happy to pay the price scribbled on the masking tape affixed to the object. Matt, on the other hand, loves to negotiate. For him, bargaining an item down from fifty cents to twenty-five cents means he's successfully talked himself into a 50 percent discount. I'd rather avoid the haggling and pay the extra quarter.

But, like a three-year-old, I don't always react in the smartest way when I'm told I can't do something. If he thought I couldn't do something, then I'd do it well just to prove him wrong. I'm your typical example of a person who bites off more than they can chew. And I'll chew and chew and chew until I choke. Deadly combination.

I quickly convinced Matt that I was serious about managing the property. He'd been encouraging me to learn how to speak up to people and saw becoming a landlord as the perfect opportunity to do so. I like how if I want to make a decision on my own, such as renting out this property, he'll support me. I also like that if I don't want to make a decision, he'll help me talk through it until I arrive at a conclusion. But for me the decision to become a landlord seemed simple enough: you find tenants; you evict them if they don't pay the rent; you call a professional when something breaks. And then you sit back and watch the dollars roll in. I got greedy, imagining the rental dollars and the rising property value. We had already made quite a bit on his house over the past five years. Who knew where its price point would be in three more years? I thought of all the money we'd end up with, how we could buy a cabin in the north woods. I imagined myself as an entrepreneur, buying up properties left and right, perhaps a fourplex even. All I had to do was find the right tenants. And cash the monthly checks that rolled in, of course.

We finally found tenants: a young married couple from New York City. She seemed efficient, sharp, organized; he spoke with a thick Brooklyn accent and punctuated each sentence with his hands. And I liked them. She reminded me of my friends from New York City with her thick, dark, curly hair, her body slender to the point where you'd think she lived off cigarettes. He was bulky like a boxer, an inch or so shorter than she was, with thick lips he bit down on too much. She worked as a financial adviser; he worked as a trader. They reminded me of a louder, less trusting version of who I was when I had first moved from New York City to Minneapolis. Back then I hadn't realized how much trust and goodwill still meant to most Minnesotans. But while living in New York, I felt everybody—from the vendor who picked bottles out of the garbage can and refilled them with tap water to the guy who advertised low-fat tuna salad that was made with regular mayonnaise—was out to screw me, so I could understand why they wanted every last thing in writing. But I knew they'd take great care of the property. Already, she had asked if she could paint the kitchen a neutral color to brighten it and lay new sod over some of the brown spots in our backyard. I was excited for them to move in.

But, of course, right after they moved in, all sorts of things went wrong: water pooled in the basement; a crack began forming in the faucet and eventually it began spurting out like a hose, strengthening as the crack grew; the man who installed the new furnace broke the water heater and then we had to replace that, too. And for every problem, I had to call Matt. I didn't know who fixed what. Sometimes, even he didn't know who fixed what, union rules seemed so tight. Because of union rules the plumber wouldn't touch the plugged drain. "You'll have to call Roto-Rooter for that," he said. I was beginning to wonder if every appliance had its own maintenance person. And so a chain started: with every problem, the tenants called me, and whenever they called, I called Matt, and then after I hung up with him, I called whomever he recommended, in addition to our tenants. I began to feel like a switchboard service.

When the garbage disposal stopped up, they called me four times in an hour between six and seven p.m. on a Friday night. "We've had to cancel our plans," they said, because the dishwasher wouldn't drain, and immediately I felt guilty.

"If they want to sit home because there are dirty dishes in the sink, then that's their problem," Matt said. "We can fix it in the morning." I like how he separates himself from issues. He decides what's fair and then doesn't second-guess himself. Sometimes I think I spend too much time trying to see the other point of view, which paralyzes me from making a decision. But soon the tenants realized that I was incapable of making a decision and began to call Matt directly, his cell phone ringing during client lunches and meetings.

And so when their lease expired a year later, both Matt and I were ready to sell the property. We decided to sell it ourselves so that we wouldn't have to pay a Realtor a commission, and, as part of our original deal, I was in charge of it. Only I didn't know where to start. "Please get the windows washed, the basement painted, the dirt sprayed off the siding, and the toilet fixed," Matt said. I sweated while pounding in a For Sale by Owner sign into the front yard. Knowing that for each month our property sat empty we'd have to carry two mortgages made me nervous. What on earth had possessed me to think that I could manage two properties, when I had as much difficulty as I did running ours alone?

I also didn't take into account how our tenants would feel about us showing our property while they were still living there. Every day, two or three Realtors called me at work saying they were in the area and would like to use our lockbox to show their clients the property. But, legally, I had to give our tenants some advance notice. So I'd call our tenants, who had two weeks left in their lease, to schedule a day and a time, but often missed a sales opportunity, as Realtors were on to other properties in the area by then. And so I asked our tenants if we could show our property at any time while they were at work with the understanding that it wouldn't be clean. They said no; in all cases they wanted twenty-four hours' notice to clean. I couldn't understand what the big deal was; just stick your dirty dishes under the sink, your laundry in a hamper, and forget about the food crumbs on the kitchen floor that nobody notices anyway. As a peacemaker, I usually want a solution that works for everyone, but in the real world, that doesn't happen very often. Our polite e-mail exchange quickly grew hostile. I felt torn between their needs and my desperation to sell the property and impress Matt. Whenever my computer beeped, indicating an e-mail had arrived in my inbox, I felt sick. Was it a bitter e-mail from them, saying a showing tomorrow wouldn't work, which meant another battle I'd have to fight? Or was it an optimistic one from Matt, asking if we had any offers on the property yet, for which he'd receive a disappointing reply? Or was it from my manager, asking why I hadn't completed a project to which I'd been assigned? I couldn't take the tension, the second-guessing, or the guilt. And so that night, I broke down.

"Dear, let's just hire a Realtor," Matt says. "Sometimes the extra money you spend is worth it if it reduces stress in your life." I'm immediately comforted by his words. Matt is more than willing to pitch in, to protect me when I need it. The point of marriage is to have a spouse upon whom you can rely, who will listen to you, support you, and take your side, no matter what the circumstances. It's okay to ask your spouse for help. You can't always do everything by yourself. In life, you don't move forward if you don't recognize your shortcomings. Why waste an extraordinary amount of time and effort trying to become better at them?

At times, Matt may know me better than I know myself. He's right; I'll probably never be a good landlord. Negotiating, bargaining, and haggling are just too stressful for me. But you know what? I don't care. We all have our limitations.

Together we work as a team to sell our property. Matt negotiates with our Realtor and tenants, while I pick up the smaller tasks, like scheduling appointments and dropping off the paperwork. And while that wasn't the role I originally wanted—nor is it the role he wanted—what we find is that it works for us. And our house sells. As we drink some wine to celebrate, Matt lovingly teases, "Do you still want that fourplex?"

"Only if you manage it," I say.

FORTY-TWO

Stop Snapping at Me

It takes two flints to make a fire.
—Louisa May Alcott

E arly one morning, while lounging in bed, I hear Matt talking to himself in the shower. Talking isn't entirely accurate. He's enunciating, pacing, articulating, and controlling his breathing. Soon he leaves for a two-week trial for which he has been preparing for over the past three months. And he wants his arguments to be perfect. I enjoy eavesdropping on him, hearing his voice above the spray of the shower. He sounds so intelligent, so determined to win over the jury while delivering an impassioned speech.

"Dammit!" I hear him yell, and I know I caused it. Whenever he gets frustrated, he lets out one sharp and colorful word. I just remembered that I took his shampoo from his shower before taking my bath and forgot to return it. I get up like a whipped puppy and retrieve the squeeze bottle from my bathroom for him.

He answers my light rap on his bathroom door. "Please put it back next time," he says sharply, his face and hair speckled with drops of water. I wince, handing him the shampoo. Sometimes Matt speaks with razor blade edges to his words.

One of Matt's paralegals asked if it was difficult for me when Matt was gone for extended trials. While I do miss him, his absence is not as hard as that week at home together before his plane departs. When Matt loses control at work, as he attempts to balance his own work along with his trial team's demands, he seeks control at home. Plus, he's exhausted, having worked past midnight for several nights in a row to prepare his client's case. Overworked and overtired, he's quick to criticize if there are flecks of food in the kitchen sink or a lightbulb is out. And now, as he comes into the bedroom to dress for work, I try to calm him by rubbing the back of his neck. "Don't do that!" he snaps.

"You're such a bully," I say, and get up out of bed, wondering how I could have married somebody who can be so insensitive to my needs. Right now, there is a complete disconnect between us, both because of the long hours he's been working and because his mind is preoccupied with work when he is at home. When I ask him a simple question I have to repeat it, because he never hears it the first time. And the second time I ask, I am so frustrated that I practically yell at him.

Brenda snaps at Mike when there is work to be done around the house and she finds him lying on the couch watching television. This is his routine: after work, he showers, they eat dinner, which he sometimes prepares, and then he turns on the television while she cleans up the kitchen. "I get so frustrated when he just sits there," Brenda says, because she sees household projects that need to be done. But what she sometimes forgets is that Mike, as a painter, has a physical job. Unlike her, he doesn't sit at a desk all day or have coffee breaks. Rather he spends ten hours on his feet, climbing up and down a two hundred-pound ladder that he must move from wall to wall. And so, when he returns home, he doesn't have the physical energy required to mow the lawn. She's learning to be more accepting of his downtime, to be more supportive of him when he has an especially hard day, and he's learning to go just a bit longer—getting in another task or two—before he calls it quits for the night.

And so I am trying to support Matt by picking up my pace during this last week before his trial. For his peace of mind, I've kept the house cleaner than usual, vacuuming every other day, making sure no pots or pans are left in the sink overnight to soak. I've taken on some of his chores, like picking up the dry cleaning, since he's working longer hours.

Now, as he looks through his closet, trying to figure out which suits he should take with him, I lie on the bed, attempting to make conversation. But he's distracted and forgetful and doesn't answer half my questions. He's focused on packing, on making sure he has the right mix of clothing laid out in his suitcase.

"Where is my shirt?" he asks.

"Which shirt?"

"The long-sleeved one. I put it in the laundry basket yesterday."

I think for a moment. "I must have left a load in the dryer," I say. I've been known to forget a load in the washing machine long enough that it starts to smell moldy or in the dryer until it wrinkles.

"How hard is it to remember to get the clothes out of the dryer?" he asks.

I can't deal with him barking at me every two minutes. "I forgot I had a load in the dryer, okay!" I yell. "I did three loads. I washed your darks, your whites, and the bedsheets. So I'm sorry that I forgot one stupid load in the dryer!" I'm crying now, trying to catch my breath between tears. I hate when my eyes blur over. I feel like I'm drooling. But I've never had a good poker face. When I feel an emotion, you see it.

"I'm sorry," he says. "I shouldn't get on you like that. I know you do a lot around here." And I know he is sorry, and I'm sorry, too. I shouldn't be overly sensitive to him. Although Matt isn't pleasant to be around right now, his irritability is a temporary state. I need to remember that, and disarm him, defusing the tension that exists in our household, rather than allowing his irritability to cause us to fight. It's not always your spouse's behavior that tears you apart; sometimes it's your reaction to it. At moments like these, there's not enough room for both of our problems and needs. And so I sit there quietly as he finishes packing, trying to forget that I feel hurt.

FORTY-THREE

The Other Woman: Matt's Assistant

*Make it thy business to know thyself, which is the
most difficult lesson in the world.*
—Miguel de Cervantes Saavedra

ast Saturday, Matt flew to Delaware for a two-week trial.
At night, after dinner but before his team gathered in the
conference room, he called me. And he sounded so worn out.
He spoke less than usual and without his boyish enthusiasm. He
didn't tell me about the trial's progression or the testimony of
the expert witness with whom he was working. Instead, as I re-
counted my day and my challenges at work, he simply listened
and gave a tired response to whatever I said.

So I decided to send him a surprise floral arrangement to cheer
him up. I called his assistant, Barb, for his address in Delaware. "I
just sent him some cookies," she said, and I stared at the phone in
my hand. I've had her assortment of cookies, which she bakes for
Matt every year at Christmas. They don't look like those deformed
chocolate chip cookies you bake in your oven or those sugar cookies you roll out on your counter, part of which burn because
you've rolled them too thin. They look like store-bought ones, in

different colors and shapes, some with sprinkles and frosting, all with the perfect texture. How do you compete with home-baked cookies?

I have no hard feelings toward Barb. She is incredibly nice and generous. She forwards me Matt's travel itinerary when I ask for it and reminds him of appointments—important ones like my birthday—that he has with me. But sometimes I think that Barb knows how to meet Matt's needs better than I do. They work together fluidly. She anticipates his needs: she knows that his most productive time for phone calls and paperwork is in the morning, so she schedules his appointments for the afternoon; she knows that he prefers to fly Northwest and that his favorite hotel in Dallas is the Fairmont; and she knows that for lunch he likes the spicy chicken pizza and an order of fresh fruit from D'Amico & Sons. And Matt likes that she takes the initiative. Because of her diligence, he is more productive at work with less to worry about. With her organizational skills, she creates a comfort zone for him at work that he definitely doesn't get at home. Half the time I don't remember to turn our oven off after I use it. Only when I feel warmth radiating from it do I realize that I've left it on. And Matt is the sort of man who requires an entire support staff to help him keep track of his car keys, his cell phone, and his wallet. When our plants needed to be watered, he actually searched the house for me to tell me to water them instead of grabbing the watering can, filling it, and watering them himself. So when he jokes that we should hire Barb to run our household, I'm not entirely sure he's kidding.

I know Matt is struggling with his own expectations of who I am in marriage. He always thought his future wife would care as much as he does about creating a home environment that reflects his personality, organized and efficient. He'd be thrilled if "we"—that is I, since he doesn't have time—kept our linen closet organized, our pantry streamlined, and our beds perfectly made. But our home reflects my personality, comfortable and creative and chaotic. Our towels lay on top of our sheets and sweatshirts, our canned goods are haphazardly stuffed on a shelf, and our beds, when they are made, show lumps beneath the comforters. I know that at times Matt finds our disorganized home stressful. But I don't want to package myself in a traditional role. That's not who I am. And Matt knew I had no desire to become a traditional wife—so why does he suddenly assume that postwedding, watering our houseplants is my responsibility? And why do I feel an internal pressure to change into the sort of wife who thrives on maintaining a comfortable home for her husband?

A day later, I call Matt to find out if he likes the floral arrangement I sent. "What flowers?" he asks. "All I received were cookies from Barb, which were really good. I shared them with the trial team." I imagine Matt passing the cookies around the conference room telling everybody what a great assistant he has. I call the floral company and discover that the flowers were lost in transit. Nobody, including the express shipping service they used, can track them down. And so Matt ends up with nothing from me, while I end up with an apology and a fifteen-dollar gift certificate.

What I'm learning is that there are a lot of people out there who are better than I am at all sorts of domestic chores, but that doesn't make them a better wife than I am. I have my strengths, too: every day, I strive to improve our marriage and make it emotionally rich. I discourage righteousness and encourage tolerance. I'm compassionate toward others. And I have a calming effect on Matt; I help him enjoy all of those little moments that make up life. It's okay to be me. In fact, it's more than okay.

While I'll always try to do what I can to make Matt's life easier, I can't do it at my own expense or put it ahead of what is important to me. I won't be satisfied with my life—or our marriage—by simply doing what Matt wants me to do or becoming who he'd like me to be. I enjoy life when I'm doing what I like to do, like writing. And when I have a positive outlook on my life, I feel good about our marriage.

I'm not always going to meet Matt's expectations or his needs, and he will have to learn to accept that. He prefers not to be distracted by the little things in life, but what he needs to understand is that I'm not so different from him. I want to focus on the big things in my life, too. And so when he leaves his dishes on the kitchen counter in the morning, I point out where our dishwasher is, informing him that both of us need to learn to be self-sufficient, not just me.

FORTY-FOUR

Do You Believe?

One religion is as true as another.

—Robert Burton

very month, Matt donates a portion of his salary to the Catholic Church. One morning, as he is reviewing our monthly statement from them, he remarks, "Dear, I think we should increase our donation." The standard, he says, is 10 percent of your income. Currently, we do not give that much to the Church, but Matt thinks that we are in a position to increase our donation. And when he gives to the Church, he trusts that his money will be used wisely or dispersed among the people who need it the most.

While we both feel that it is our duty to give back what we can to the community, the Church is not my favorite institution to which to donate. With all of the sex abuse scandals, the cover-ups that have followed, and the alleged financial settlements to victims, I cannot justify increasing our donation. I refuse to bail the Church out of its legal troubles when our money could assist AIDS research or feed starving children.

How do other newlyweds resolve their religious differences? Matt and I are both Catholic, but we have very different ideas of what that means as well as what sort of role religion should play in our marriage. When we first married, I didn't think our religious differences would be an issue until we had to negotiate how to raise our children. But here we are, arguing over what seems like the bottom line for so many things: money.

Before I met Matt, I never gave money to the Church, and I rarely attended. I had been raised Catholic but had tired of its need for intellectual conformity. In church, I felt uncomfortable, as if your purpose as a Catholic was to judge and be judged. And, for me, judging a person before you've walked in their shoes is one of man's greatest sins. That's not to say I'm above passing judgment. I've been guilty of talking behind people's backs on more than one occasion. But to do so in the name of God seems sacrilegious to me.

Religion felt like an angry and hostile corrective measure. I refused to be part of a congregation that blindly nodded along with whatever a priest said. I believe that you should question everything. I know that for some adhering to the Catholic Church's rules—or any religion's rules—guarantees life after death. But I trusted my own internal moral compass. And so I grew up separating God from religion. Religion, for me, was about compassion and empathy, as simple as, "Do onto others as you would have done unto you." I liked thinking a greater power existed to which we must answer, that the little acts of kindness and selflessness that we perform in this life matter. I saw religion as a sort of universal spirituality or goodness, a safety net that would stop life's hardships from falling solely onto my own shoulders. I considered myself a "cafeteria-style" Catholic. I took from the Church whatever lessons I felt were appropriate and left the rest.

And then I met Matt, who didn't share my cynicism about the Catholic Church. He focused on its positives and attempted to adhere to many of its doctrines. At first, I considered this a strike against him. But shortly after we began dating, he convinced me to go to church with him. At first I told myself that I would go as a favor to him, that religion and its symbolisms and tradition meant nothing to me. As I sat there in church, I dispassionately dissected religion and what it meant and began to see it in some cases as a valuable form of social construct. It provided a framework in which to teach morals and values. But that was as far as I went. I felt nothing as I bowed my head and recited the prayers I had unthinkingly memorized as a child.

When the collection basket was passed, I turned my head when Matt put money into it. Secretly, I thought he donated because he thought it'd assure his place in heaven, that it was nothing more than a bribe to a higher power. Out of sensitivity to his spiritual needs, though, I left him alone about his monthly donation, and I didn't protest when he continued giving it to the Church after we married. But now that he wants to increase the amount, I have to speak up.

"Why do you want to increase our contribution?" I ask. What frustrates me is that Matt, who with all other charities asks fifty questions before removing a dollar bill from his wallet, gives unquestioningly to the Church. "I'm not giving them our hard-earned money to pay off their lawsuits."

"I don't want our money to pay for that, either," Matt says. "But you're overlooking all of the good that has been done by the Catholic Church." At this moment, I sense how strongly he feels about increasing our donation. And I'm sure he feels how strongly I am against it.

I know that you have to respect your spouse's faith and have tolerance for it. I firmly believe that if something is important to your spouse, then you need to make it important to you, too. But what I find frustrating is that Matt doesn't know why he believes some of the things that he does. I understand that in religion, you reach a point where you can't prove anything beyond it, like the existence of God. That is what faith is about. But I want him to be an informed Catholic, to know why he must go to church on Sundays, why he's supposed to donate 10 percent of his salary to the Church, and why he is a Catholic rather than another religion.

And so, I asked him, "Do you think you're any better off in God's eyes than I am if you don't know what you believe or why?"

"I never thought of it that way," he said. And he began reading the Bible that night.

That wasn't the reaction I had expected from him. But, as I lay in bed beside him—he was still reading the Bible—I realized that my assessment of him isn't always fair. There are depths within him that I do not know, that I have not yet reached. And I'm only, through time, starting to uncover them. I'm amazed how much lies beneath his skin. Sometimes it's just a function of time; he has such a busy life that he doesn't have the luxury to stay in his head like I do. But a lot of what's tucked inside him is starting to surface while we're together, and I'm touched by the depth to which our relationship has gone. Watching him read, I wondered if I was just as guilty as I had accused him of being, because I had stopped thinking about religion, too.

Soon, I found that I was beginning to search for meaning and understanding in it all, too. What did I believe? Did I really believe nothing at all? Or had I, like I had accused Matt, simply stopped thinking about it?

Now I regularly attend church with Matt on Sundays. I have to admit that I've been impressed with our parish. Our priest tackles the tough subjects—like the sex abuse scandals—that have rocked the Catholic Church. He is more like a teacher than a judge; he explains why the Church believes what it does, and I leave mass with a sense of peace, of goodness, that I've never felt in a church before. But I still don't know how I feel about many of the Catholic Church's doctrines. While Matt and my beliefs may never be the same, we're learning to become more tolerant of each other's position.

I still do not feel we should increase our donation to the Church, but we come up with a fair compromise. We agree to help pay for one student's tuition at the Catholic school. That way I know our money is accounted for, and he feels he is doing what is spiritually right.

FORTY-FIVE

Good-bye Single Gal

Talk not of wasted affection, affection never was wasted.
—Henry Wadsworth Longfellow

My best friend from high school, Lisa, called me while I was in Tucson, Arizona, visiting Matt's parents, to say that her husband, George, was killed in Iraq. I got the call while sitting in the backseat of Matt's parents' van, waiting for his dad to emerge from Home Depot.

Not Lisa, I thought. *This couldn't happen to her.* Ever since I had known her, what had been most important to her was a family—a husband, a home, and children to fill it.

I felt numb, too shocked to speak, so I climbed from the van and wandered toward the sunlight with the cell phone pressed to my ear until Matt's mom grabbed my arm.

Lisa and I became best friends at eleven years of age after meeting at my Little League softball team. She loved basketball; I loved soccer. She was tall; I was of average height. She was sweet; I could be impertinent. We were inseparable in high school, but in college we grew apart.

Our sophomore year of college, she had begun dating George, a Cornell football player. I worried about her. Unlike most of my friends, she dreamed not of a career or a higher education but of becoming a wife and a mother, what I considered a cop-out on life. Anybody could become a wife and a mother, but what was the point? In those roles, you ceaselessly cooked and cleaned and washed dishes, while your mind eroded.

As she dreamed of her wedding day, I dreamed of moving to New York City to "make it." There was no way that I was going to let a man stand between me and my life goals. And I let Lisa know that I thought she was too young to marry. At the time, I didn't realize how much my words hurt her or how much she had wanted my approval. I thought I was doing what was right, that I could save her from a future that didn't look bright to me. But, at twenty-four, she married George anyway. I felt that I had somehow failed her. I had tried so hard to get her to recognize her potential, and still, she chose marriage, a life of subservience, over freedom.

We stopped talking shortly thereafter. There wasn't a final blowup between us or harsh parting words. There was just nothing left to say to each other. She didn't understand my life in New York City, as I struggled with graduate school and a low-paying full-time job and credit card debt. I couldn't communicate to her how helpless I felt scrambling to come up with the money to buy subway tokens. And I had little desire to understand her life and what she was sacrificing working two jobs to help George through graduate school. Years went by. I thought of her only in passing, preoccupied with my own life.

And then, five years later, I got an e-mail from her. She had given birth to her long-awaited baby, a little girl, and was living in Germany with George, who had joined the army as a commissioned armor officer. Her e-mail was friendly but reserved, factual without any emotion. And I responded to it, as I would anybody else's, not letting on to the hurt and betrayal I felt about how our friendship had ended.

Our e-mail exchange continued. We asked polite questions and gave polite answers. I had been dating Matt for over a year and knew he was about to propose. When he did, Lisa sent an e-mail in which she responded saying she felt we could finally be friends again; I'd understand her life now. And while I have to admit that I did have a better understanding and a new respect for what she wanted out of life, I felt her e-mail dismissed all I had accomplished in the interim. I responded, apologizing for any pain that I had caused her, but also explaining how her behavior had hurt me. A week later, we had worked through our issues. We were two different people with two different needs, but we had matured enough to build a friendship that was flexible enough for both of us.

It's true that you never know what will blindside you on a hot Sunday afternoon while you're debating whether pine or maple laminate would work better in your living room. When I saw that unrecognizable area code come through on the cell phone, I was annoyed at the interruption, thinking the call was from a telemarketer. But there was Lisa's breathless voice. For over an hour, we talked. I felt sick for her, for this chasm in her life that George's death has created, for having to tell her three-year-old that Daddy was hurt and won't be coming home.

Matt flew to Tucson to be with me, but he couldn't provide the comfort I needed. I needed to see Lisa, to hug her, to make sure that she was okay. The funeral was to be in Utica, New

York. I told Lisa I'd meet her there. Both Matt and I scrambled to get flights. I flew from Phoenix to Detroit to Elmira, New York, where my mom picked me up and drove me to Utica. Matt's plane was scheduled to fly from Phoenix to Minneapolis to Rochester, New York, where he'd rent a car and drive to Utica. As he wouldn't arrive until morning, I went to the wake alone.

I saw Lisa for the first time standing in the receiving line. She looked pale and thin, like her heart leaked the fuel required for her body to run. I thought if I touched her, she wouldn't feel it through her numbness. But I hugged her anyway, and she crumpled. I could feel some of her pain sinking into my body, and I ached everywhere. I knew when I released her, all of the pain would settle back into her frail body. There was nothing I could do to help her. The foundation upon which she had built her life was missing a critical cornerstone, and now the structure was sinking. So I let her go and sat down in one of the pews.

Nine months before George left for Iraq, he and Lisa struggled with his departure to a war zone. It hurt him to know that he'd miss a year of his young daughter's life. His father had died from Agent Orange exposure in Vietnam when George was a young boy. And George feared he might leave his wife a widow and his daughter fatherless. But duty called. So, before he left, he began to pull away from Lisa, afraid of causing her the sort of pain his father's death had caused him. As George spent more time at the office, she ached for herself and her daughter. She couldn't understand why he wouldn't want to spend more time with them now, when there was no guarantee he'd come back from Iraq. And so she called me from Fort Worth, Texas, where George was stationed, to talk. I invited her to come visit me in Minneapolis, and, soon afterward, she and her adorable little girl arrived.

"I can't believe how domestic you are," she said, and I laughed. I had developed an obsessive need to keep our countertops clean. I did feel like my mom having a dishrag attached to my hand. And through her eyes I could see that I was settling into my new role as a wife. But what surprised me was that I didn't consider myself weak or subservient; I was merely doing my part in keeping our household running smoothly. I was starting to accept that I was no longer the independent single gal I had longed to be for so long. I had found my identity in marriage and liked who I was, simply a better, stronger, smarter version of my old self.

And I couldn't believe how much Lisa had grown in her marriage, how she had truly found herself. She headed up a family readiness group for the army, organizing monthly meetings. She did fund-raising for military balls and charities and sent holiday packages to the soldiers. Fathers and mothers, wives and husbands of enlisted men and women and junior officers depended on her. What I was starting to realize was that it was people like Lisa who stitch together the fabric of our society that make our world a better place for all of us.

But I did secretly wonder if her relationship would survive with George withdrawing from it. I felt proud of the marriage Matt and I had created together. We had finally figured out our relationship, bending for each other at every turn. He'd bring home flowers, and I'd trim their edges before putting them in a vase on our dining room table. Our home was peaceful and loving and comfortable. And what I had with Matt, I wanted Lisa to have with George, too. Only at this moment, George, with his fears, was unable to give her more than his physical presence. And so I asked her what made her stay with him.

"No relationship will ever be perfect," Lisa said dismissively. "Six years down the road you may be in my shoes. You never know what's around the next corner. You need to keep in mind why you married your husband. Obviously, there was something—and there still is—that you love about him very much."

I wasn't sure what I thought of her advice. Divorce, I think, is terribly hard. But do you want to spend your life in an unhappy marriage? And, if not, at what point do you move on?

But, for Lisa, her marriage was her greatest investment. Her commitment was more important than how she felt about George right then. There'd always be highs and lows, she said, but what was important was that you showed up each day and did your best, and eventually you'd clear the fog between you. And so she returned home ready to fight for her marriage. "I know you're scared," she said to George. "I'm scared, too. But ask yourself, 'What do I want my daughter's memories of me to be?' If you keep working so much, she won't have any of you." He thought about her words. And then he saw clearly how much pain he was causing Lisa and their daughter. He worked to create invaluable memories for them. He started spending more time with them, taking them to the park and to the zoo. He made videotapes of himself reading bedtime stories for their daughter. And Lisa accepted and forgave him for the pain that he caused her without question. "The pain you go through together is the glue that holds you together for the happy fifty-year marriage," she said. And her heart broke when George left for Iraq.

At George's calling hours, I was horrified by how many people ignored Lisa in the receiving line, going straight for his mother. One woman literally elbowed Lisa out of the way. Didn't anybody have any idea of what Lisa had built with George, of what George had built with Lisa, and how long and hard they had fought to protect it? Doesn't anybody respect the institution of marriage anymore?

That night, I, along with some of Lisa's army and college friends, went back to her in-laws' home. It was the first time I had been somewhere with Lisa and felt I didn't belong. Her military life had been so different from my civilian one. When I asked her where she planned to live after moving off base, she said she was considering living near a friend in Ohio whose husband had served with George. She said she needed to be near somebody who "knew what it all meant." Although she hadn't directed that comment toward me, I felt it deep within. She was right; I didn't know what it all meant. I barely knew her anymore. While I'll always love Lisa like a sister, there are so many gaps created by time and space and geography between us now. I wasn't there for monumental events of her life like the birth of her daughter. I'd never seen her home in Germany or been on an army base with her. I didn't know the routine of her day. I was her past, struggling to fit in with her present and future.

"I never thought I'd be widowed at thirty-one," she said, flipping through a photo album of letters from George as well as condolence letters she had put together for her daughter. "I am so glad that George died knowing how very, very much I loved him. I loved him with my whole heart."

I left her then to meet Matt at our hotel room. He arrived around two a.m. I was so relieved to see a familiar face, somebody who would help relieve my pain for Lisa and also my loneliness at having lost her myself years ago. As I held him, I realized that he was my best friend now. Through Lisa, I had learned that my friendship with him wouldn't always be easy or uncomplicated. But for all of the energy I've poured into maintaining friendships over the years, my friendship with Matt is the one I really have to focus on. He is my best friend, my present and my future. He is the one who will be there for me.

He has seen me at my best and my worst, and loves me through it all.

Early the next morning, Matt and I rose to dress for the funeral. I hugged him as soon as he stepped from the shower, grateful that he was alive. We ate a quick breakfast, our stomachs jittery, and then drove to the church. We sat down in one of the pews. I was amazed by how many lives George had touched. Men flew in from all over the country—Alaska, even—to pay their respects. And for the first time I saw George as Lisa did: he discovered a Roman fort in southern Germany by begging for helicopter rides from the medevac pilots; he got permission from the farmer who owned the land to search it for pottery, which he found; through the use of satellite imagery he discovered another Roman fort in Syria. He wrote articles on his discoveries, which he then published. But, even more, I was amazed by the greatness I saw in Lisa. I knew how much pain she had quietly absorbed out of love for her family over the years, and how much more it would absorb on behalf of her daughter.

It seemed so unfair that what Lisa wanted most in life she had lost. And it seemed so unfair that it took her terrible loss to make me appreciate what she had had. All of my fears about her future before she married didn't hurt like my worries for her now. Nothing you do out of love is a waste. Love, whether for your spouse, your friends, or your family, is all that there is in life. It's not a sign of weakness or inadequacy; it isn't a crutch, but truly a gift. There's nothing more difficult than learning to trust and be vulnerable, than removing layers of self-protection that took years to put in place. It is true that your heart is your strongest muscle, the one that is capable of giving you the most joy and the most pain.

Matt and I prayed for George and for Lisa and for their

daughter. We held hands and cried. And then we watched Lisa follow her husband's casket out the door, all alone.

I can't fix Lisa's life. I can't be there as she struggles, hoping this hour will be better than the last, that this day will be better than yesterday, that next week will be better than this one. But she has given me a great gift. She has taught me to open my eyes and see love for the amazing gift that it is.

FORTY-SIX

Number One Fan

*There is an unfortunate disposition in man to
attend much more to the faults of his companions
that offend him, than to their perfections
which please him.*
—Greville

One Saturday night, Matt and I meet friends at a bar for happy hour. We stand on an outdoor patio, enjoying the light breeze and afternoon sun while sipping mojitos. I overhear a woman, who is talking to a friend of mine, say, "It's kind of like the big bookstore chain pushing the little store out of business." I want to put my hand over her mouth, but it's too late. Matt has heard her as well, and his reaction, like an electric shock, is instantaneous.

"Speaking of which," he says to her, and now I want to put my hands over my ears. "Have you heard about the Amazon Bookstore?" She shakes her head. He's immovable, reveling in the attention. If a waitress asked Matt if he wanted "ham on the side," his response would be, "Did you say Amazon?" Because that case is his claim to fame, his inexhaustible fifteen minutes.

If the entire world's a stage, then Matt knows how to capture the limelight. People energize him. Around them he's like a windup toy with his relentless energy and flashes of enthusiasm. It doesn't matter if you're five years old or sixty, if your English is poor, or if you're deaf in one ear, he'll still share his success with you with the same boyish zeal—but always without arrogance, always with a willing ear, for which you'll inevitably find him charming. And I'll find him annoyingly embarrassing.

As he begins his narration, I realize that we're both telling this story, only he's speaking out loud while I'm simply mouthing the words. I've heard this story so many times that my mind is acting like a teleprompter that I can't turn off. With each word that flicks by I know which gesture of his will follow.

Here's his story: One Friday night, after barhopping with friends and drinking just a bit too much, he took a cab home. The next morning, as he was jogging downtown to pick up his truck, he noticed the shop front for the Amazon Bookstore. And so he went in.

"I said to the clerk, 'I didn't know that Amazon.com was based in Minneapolis,'" Matt says. "She looked up at me annoyed. 'We're not Amazon.com,' she said tartly. 'We've been in business for twenty years.' And then she said that there was nothing they could do about the name confusion. But I disagreed. I said that even though the law wasn't clear, the Amazon Bookstore had a strong trademark case." I roll my eyes.

As his fervor builds, his face inches closer to the woman at the bar. "The owner of the bookstore called me the next day," he says. "And so we worked it out so that Amazon Bookstore could sue Amazon.com without having to pay any legal fees." The lawsuit lasted for about a year, during which time Matt was quoted in the *Wall Street Journal* and *Time* magazine, while his picture ran on the AP wire. It was then that I met him, right when he began receiving awards: Lawsuit of the Year, Forty under 40, and Rising Star. New lawyers at his firm told him that they had studied his case in law school. Back then, I was intimidated by his success, threatened even, but I've since adjusted to it. And now, three years later, I'm annoyed by anything related to it.

I know that Anne finds Pete embarrassing at times. While she loves his sense of humor—she finds him hysterical—she blushes when he jokes with people he doesn't know who have no context for his humor. "We'll be shopping, and he'll tell the cashier that he's going to sue her when she accidentally scans in an item twice," she says. "But she doesn't know that he's a lawyer or that he's joking. She doesn't know how funny he can be." The cashier just stares blankly back at him. Anne can empathize with the cashier; when she first met Pete, she didn't like him because she thought he was making fun of her. But she's starting to accept Pete for who he is. While his behavior may embarrass her at times, the laughter they share solidifies their marriage. And she wouldn't want him to change his sense of humor one bit.

Now, at the bar, the woman asks Matt, "So what was the outcome of the trial?" I've had enough.

"It was three years ago," I interject, before he can respond. "Can't you get over it already?" My words come out harsher than I intend, and, right away, I wish I could take them back. But my interjection lingers there. The woman frowns and looks at her feet. And Matt looks disappointed.

I bite my lip. The truth is that I am proud of Matt, of who he is and all of his successes. But that is not what I'm conveying to him at this moment, and his positive traits—his eloquence and charm—are not what I'm focusing on. Marriage should be your safe zone; you shouldn't use it to cause pain or test your spouse. You should use it to support one another. Nothing is gained during a verbal attack, except a momentary rush of superiority. But much is lost, like love, trust, and respect. His successes are not my failures. What do you gain by competing with your spouse?

"I'm sorry," I say, taking a step back, trying to gracefully exit this conversation. I silently vow not to say a bad word about Matt again in public, knowing that love, as a language, takes practice. Even if Matt is still telling this story to our grandchildren when we're seventy years old, I'll let him because it makes him happy. Now when people ask Matt if he's ever worked on an interesting case, I say, "Tell them about the Amazon Bookstore case." And his eyes sparkle.

FORTY-SEVEN

What Makes You a Woman?

I'll walk where my own nature would be leading;
it vexes me to choose another guide.

—Emily Brontë

When are you having kids?" Matt's cousin asks us, and I don't respond at first. I uncomfortably shift my gaze to Matt. Inside, I seethe. Since when did this question become socially acceptable? Friends, coworkers, acquaintances, and even shop clerks ask me it. I was so relieved when I finally had an answer to the question, "When are you getting married?" And now this. Silently, I think of all sorts of retorts that in reality I'd never say: *I hate kids, I'm infertile,* or *We've decided to breed puppies instead.*

Another cousin shakes her head and laughs. "Don't listen to them," she says. "As soon as you have one kid, they'll be asking you when you're going to have another." She lifts her second baby for me to see, and her words somehow make the question feel less invasive. The attention shifts off us and onto the cooing baby who's drooling and waggling his arms.

Only Matt says, "Did you notice she's not drinking?" He

winks at them, looping one arm around me. I stand there, empty-handed, staring up at his profile, furious. He knows I'm not pregnant—we're not even trying—but here he is, starting a rumor that will run through his entire family before I have a chance to drink a beer to prove that I'm not. And then I'll feel forced to explain why we're not even trying, when our reproductive affairs should be nobody's business but ours. The decision to have children should be a private one. Nobody knows what's right for us like we do. We'll be the ones waking up for the middle-of-the-night feedings or changing dirty diapers.

I admit that I'm guilty of having asked this question in the past. I assumed that having children was a natural step for most married couples. But now that I'm on the receiving end of it, the question feels incredibly personal. As much as stereotypes bother me, I do feel like childbearing is more connected to how I see myself, and how I'm seen socially, than how Matt views himself. And so, to me, this question feels critical and accusatory, with assumptions, however intended, embedded in it—that you want children, that you're somehow inferior without them, that your role in life is as a mother and wife. It feels like pressure to adapt to society's standard of what a successful marriage should look like or who you should be in it. And I have enough trouble figuring out who I am without this added pressure.

When we get home, I stalk up our front stairs into the house. Matt comes in behind me, and I whirl around to face him. "Why do you do that? You know I hate it when people ask me when we're having a baby. So why do you play with them like that? It's not funny."

He simply laughs. "It keeps them guessing," he says.

"But it's not their business. You need to tell your family to stop asking us that question." I glare at him. Matt hates when I make blanket statements about *your family*. His family is huge, and he says I shouldn't lump them together.

"They're just making polite talk," he says dismissively.

"It doesn't feel like it to me." I barely know these cousins and great-aunts who are asking these invasive questions. Without having a united front, Matt and I will never stop this line of questioning. "Even if you do not understand my feelings, you need to respect them," I say.

Later that week, I find out that both Christina and Brenda are pregnant, sharing a due date. I'm excited for both of them, especially for Brenda, who feels a baby will help bring legitimacy to her marriage, Mike's second marriage. She views the impending birth of their child as a unifying experience for Mike and her, both in their eyes and society's. With a child, she'll have her own family unit with Mike, rather than feeling like a third wheel whenever his daughter is around.

But now I feel more pressure to have a baby—not so much because my friends are pregnant, but because we are all close in age. Like your dating track, your mama track speeds up when you're over thirty, as both Christina and Brenda are, as you struggle to find that precarious balance between your biological clock and your emotional, as well as financial, readiness. And I've heard the warnings. When you're over thirty, getting pregnant can be a precise science. Forget sex. You need books, thermometers, ovulation predictor kits, and charts. And, if that doesn't work, you resort to all sorts of home remedies to try to enhance your fertility like Robitussin, grapefruit juice, and baby aspirin. Though I share in their joy, I can't help but wonder if our marriage is somehow lagging behind theirs, as Matt and I have yet to take that step forward. I know that you have to take life at your own pace. Keeping up with societal expectations or

your friends won't improve your marriage. You're better off disappointing your critics than living a life you're not ready or prepared for. But still, as I watch how much joy Brenda and
Christina experience with their pregnancies, I wonder, is it time
for Matt and me to take that next step, too?

FORTY-EIGHT

My Supportive Husband

To love someone deeply gives you strength. Being
loved by someone deeply gives you courage.

—Lao-tzu

I got a literary agent based on my fifty-page book proposal. I call Matt at work on the telephone, and he is just as thrilled as I am. Securing an agent is not easy. They only make money if they sell your book. And both of us know that usually you need an agent to approach a major publisher with a manuscript. While there are no guarantees that your agent will sell your manuscript, a good one ensures that your work will be marketed to publishers correctly and seriously considered. And I finally have one.

"You need to quit your job," Matt says without hesitation.

"What?" I stammer. I forgot that we had agreed that if I got an agent, we'd reconsider having me quit my job to pursue writing full-time.

"Give your notice today," he says. "You need to work on your book proposal." Together my agent and I will perfect my book proposal—an overview, market analysis, chapter summaries, and sample chapters—until we feel publishers can't resist it.

He's right; I should quit my day job. Why waste my energy programming Web sites when I could be pursuing my dream? But I hedge. For all of my agonizing over the past few months, I find that I simply can't quit working. I've always had my own paycheck. In high school, I steamed rice in the Cornell University cafeteria; in college, I photocopied and addressed envelopes; in graduate school, I filed microfiche in the library. If I leave the computer industry now, with its ever-changing programming languages and jobs being shipped offshore, I could be locked out of a job for months, perhaps a year, even, to come.

But what I don't admit to Matt is that I can't be completely financially dependent on him. I need a way to somehow secure myself in case our marriage doesn't work. If money is power, then how will he use his?

That night, Matt and I have a long-overdue talk about our finances. We look at his income and mine, and where we'd be if I stopped working. We talk about our financial goals and weigh those against our decision. Always conservative when it comes to money, I can't decide what we should do.

"Nothing is gained without risk," Matt says encouragingly. He gets out a yellow legal pad and a pen and jots down a few ideas. He likes to take notes to help him remember our talking points. We discuss revising our spending habits and setting a budget. He makes two columns. In one, he writes which categories are most important to us, like traveling to see family, and in the other, where we can cut, like eating out and groceries. We talk about giving ourselves a monthly allowance from which we can spend freely and unquestionably. Then we list all of our mandatory household expenditures.

"We can do this," Matt says, as I look at the notes he's scribbled down. I am comforted to know that even without an income I'll still share the responsibility of making financial decisions. There's no power struggle here. Money has become less important than our relationship.

And I'm touched by how much Matt is willing to sacrifice to support me in who I am and what I want from life. I'm delighted by the pleasure that Matt finds in my success. With his unwavering support, I start to think I can quit my job—financially and, more importantly, emotionally.

I am starting to see how lucky I am to have a supportive husband like Matt. For the first time in our marriage, I am truly ready to take my leap of faith, to throw myself headfirst and blindly into my love for Matt, with nothing but the best of intentions. I can't continue to hold back part of myself as leverage or an escape route. I can't half commit, live day to day thinking of an alternative life should this one not work. You only get as good as you give. And Matt's right; risks lead to reward in everything in life: marriage, love, and career. You need to take risks and make yourself vulnerable to allow your love, trust, and commitment to deepen. So together we work into the night setting up a writing schedule to keep time from slipping away from me. And, when we finish, I know that with his support, I can do anything.

The next morning at work, as I look around my cubicle, which is cluttered with technical documents and textbooks, its only personal touch a miniature stuffed deer that Matt won for me at the state fair, I ask myself, "Do you want this to be your home for the next twenty years?" I know the answer. Slowly I walk into my manager's office and give notice.

Two weeks later, sipping coffee at home, I realize that I feel nothing but relief having quit. I open our office windows to hear birds chirping, nested in the tree outside it. I work in my sweat-pants. I jog each morning. And I'm surprised to find that our marriage is slowly improving now that one of us is home to do the sort of chores that went undone or caused an argument before. I'm happier, less stressed from the demands of a day job, and, as a result, Matt is happier, too.

My position at work has already been filled, my projects picked up where I left off. But I know that there is one place in life in which I am irreplaceable. I pick up the phone and call Matt. I miss him.

FORTY-NINE

See Work to Do, Part II

Responsibility educates.
—Wendell Phillips

A month from our one-year anniversary, Matt and I decide to take that next big step in life as a family. Our marriage has stabilized. We have a steady income. And now that we've completed our home-remodeling project, we're ready for noise other than our own.

"You'll feel less lonely while I'm traveling," Matt says. But I need no convincing; I'm ready to commit. So on a glorious Sunday afternoon we drive to a small town two hours south of Minneapolis where we select a blond golden retriever from a litter of six.

We choose the runt, who follows Matt all over the yard, waddling on her stubby legs. She can't see very far with her undeveloped eyes, so she pokes her nose in the air for his scent. He claps to get her attention, and her tail wags. I pick her up and breathe in her sweet puppy smell, her fur fluffy and soft like a cotton ball. After her breeder bathes her, we get into the car and start our drive home, with a towel covering my lap. And she pukes on me.

Shortly after we return home, she piddles on our hardwood floor twice, but neither Matt nor I care. She brings so much life into our house I can't stop staring at her. I've often heard that before you have a child you should get a dog to teach yourself about responsibility. And now that I'm working from home I think we can easily handle the adjustment of having a puppy. Only that night, we barely sleep. We put her in her crate in the kitchen, and she shrieks so loud and for so long that I am sure she is dying.

"If you go in there, she'll do it again tomorrow night," Matt says, and I know he is right. But I worry she's caught her paw in the bars, so after a half hour I check on her. While I'm with her, she is quiet, but as soon as I walk out of the kitchen, she starts shrieking again. I try covering my head with a pillow, but that doesn't work. I'm exhausted the next day, barely able to function without a cup of coffee every few hours. By the third night, I can't take it anymore, so I break my first rule. I allow her to sleep in her kennel in the bedroom with us, and, at last, she is quiet.

I take this new addition to our family seriously. I want a well-trained dog, one who looks away from the table when we eat dinner, who doesn't jump up on or sniff our guests, who heels on command. So, in my usual manner of learning, I go to the library and check out a few books about how to raise a dog. After careful research, I give Matt guidelines for raising her: No raising your voice, because a stern correction will do; don't pet her while she's jumping up on you or you'll reinforce her bad behavior; don't feed her people food unless you put it in her dish so that she doesn't associate it with you; walk through doors first, or else she'll think she can dominate you; at all times, remember that you are the pack leader, and so act like it.

"How am I supposed to remember all of those rules?" Matt

asks, perplexed. His dog while growing up roamed freely out-doors, sleeping on the hard garage floor or in the back hall on particularly cold nights.

So I write them down for him. On the whiteboard in our kitchen, I sketch out her schedule, detailing when she should eat and relieve herself to try to make potty training quick and painless. He stares at the whiteboard as if I've written on it in hieroglyphics.

"If she goes to the bathroom in the house, why don't we just rub her nose in it?" he asks.

"Because then she won't associate the puddle on the floor with her action," I say. "She'll see the puddle as bad but won't know *why*. In the end, your actions will only make her afraid of you."

"She's a dog," he says, looking at me as if I have truly lost my mind. It's that farm mentality coming out in him. She's more than a dog to me. She's *poochie*, *my little bear*, *my love*—to Matt she's *the dog*.

During my workday, she is a constant interruption, whimper-ing to go out, nipping at my ankles to play, and ducking behind the couch to chew up my high-heel shoes. Whereas Matt would confine her to the back hall, I try to correct her behavior, replac-ing my shoes with her chew toys. I start her in obedience classes and work with her each night. Matt, lacking my patience, gives her the wrong commands and then gets frustrated when she doesn't respond to them. Or he repeats the same command over and over, until "SitSitSitSit" replaces "Sit" in her little brain, and then rewards her.

"Not like that!" I holler, whenever I catch him, afraid he'll un-ravel all of my training. I know I've turned into a horrible nag over our puppy. You need to give your spouse space to parent. But what do you do when they do everything wrong?

Nothing has convinced me that men and women are fundamentally different as much as our new puppy has. Or else Matt is deaf, and I'm just starting to realize it. He doesn't hear our puppy whimpering to go out or barking to have her food dish refilled. Nor does he feel guilty if we leave her in her crate for more than an hour or two. And I think he believes that one day she will magically be housebroken. He doesn't realize that this little puppy, with her need to shred newspapers and books to pieces, eat only what can rupture her intestines, and potty on our new carpet every twenty minutes, has started to run my life.

She'll sit next to him and whimper and, as he doesn't hear her, he'll do nothing. Downstairs I sit, cringing with each whimper. Finally, I run up. "Can't you hear that?" I ask.

"What?" he says, and strains his head like there's music playing in the background or sirens whistling down the street.

I point to the puppy, whose whimpers have been replaced with deep painful hums. "She wants to go out!" He looks at me as if I share ESP with the puppy. "Don't you hear her whimpering?"

"I didn't hear her," he says.

"How could you not? She's sitting right next to you." I open the sliding glass door for her, and she scoots out. "You can never tell me to see work to do again. As far as the puppy is concerned, you never see any work to do."

I shouldn't be so hard on Matt. Each night, he takes our puppy for a long walk on the golf course. And this small act is wonderful, as it releases some of her energy, making her just a bit easier to manage. Sometimes, if he sprints with her, she'll return home and flop at my feet.

And I know that if it were just me, our puppy would grow up afraid of everything. But Matt lets her run off leash on the golf course, free and wild, and in the house sets stricter boundaries for her. She knows with a toss of her head I will think her cute for stealing my sock and growling at it. But through Matt she has learned both *no* and *drop*. And he doesn't mind picking up the yard after her. For me, that's a big plus.

But what I'm quickly learning is that being happily married is very different from being prepared for a child. While I know that having a baby is even more demanding than having a dog—with a greater reward—what's similar is having to renegotiate every aspect of your relationship, from your careers (*who will work late and who will be home to let her out?*), to your social lives (*how long will she last in her kennel on a Saturday night?*), to your daily routine (*who will walk her each morning and feed her?*), to your differing parenting styles (*how will we potty train her?*). And I don't think Matt and I are ready for that added responsibility a child brings yet.

FIFTY

My List, My Project

I am not now
That which I have been.
—Lord Byron

There is one room in our house that still retains its original pink and purple wallpaper, and that is our kitchen. And so neither of us likes to eat in there. We'll go in there to fill our water glasses or make a sandwich but eat elsewhere. While the rest of the house feels like home to us, the kitchen doesn't.

While remodeling, we designated our kitchen as a Phase II project, which I know from my years as a programmer is a politically correct way of saying, "We'll never get to it." For a while, that was fine with both of us. I didn't want to pay the expense of having the wallpaper removed, and Matt didn't find it as offensive as I did. However, now that I'm enjoying decorating our home, I want a color theme to run throughout it. So I'm trying to push the kitchen remodel back into Phase I. I want our home to look perfectly cozy and inviting.

But Matt disagrees. "I don't want to spend any more money on contractors," he says. "Let's just keep the kitchen as it is as a reminder of how the house used to look." I can appreciate his frustration. Our contractors' final bill was significantly more than their bid. They claimed our damaged walls required more patching than they had anticipated, but we had our suspicions.

"Would you mind if I did it myself?" I ask.

"Dear, you won't finish it," he says kindly. This hurts, but he has a point. Early on in our marriage, I finished none of the major household projects I'd originally put on my list because I thought they'd be fun—like building a brick garden, organizing our box of photographs, framing our posters and paintings. Of course, I didn't realize that they weren't fun until after I'd already bought the supplies. And so I didn't follow through on hobbies like sewing, although I had bought a brand-new machine, or cooking, for which I bought all sorts of gadgets. Most tasks I completed in a haphazard way. Half our plants died under my care.

But I'm slowly becoming a more responsible person, and Matt knows it. Through him, I've learned how to stay focused and organized. On Saturday mornings, my crossed-off task list is often as long as his. Yet while he has seen my transformation, he still doesn't trust that I won't revert to some of my old habits. And, to be honest, I don't completely trust that I'll have the energy to strip all of the wallpaper in the kitchen, either. So I let the matter drop.

But the next morning, while he's at work and I'm standing in the kitchen, I impulsively lean over and rip off the top layer of the wallpaper, without its adhesive backing, from one part of the wall. I can't stop myself. Soon, all of the wallpaper is down, crumpled on the floor around me. When my adrenaline rush evaporates, I realize I've made a huge mess. I ball up the wallpaper on the floor and stuff it into our garbage container. And then I go back into the kitchen and stare at the walls, at the imprint of decorative squiggly raised lines on the wallpaper in the adhesive backing. What a nightmare it will be to scrape all of that hardened glue loose! And what will Matt's reaction be to my impulsive behavior when he walks through our front door? Will I be able to follow through on what I've started?

That night, I cringe when I hear the garage door open. Matt walks in and greets me with a kiss and a caress. He goes everywhere except for the kitchen—into the bedroom to slip into jeans, into the office to read his mail, and into the family room to catch the last of the nightly news.

Finally, I can't take it anymore. "Come with me to the kitchen," I say. He perks up, visualizing a delightful surprise like home-baked brownies.

It takes a moment for him to notice how bare the walls are. I study his face, searching for an emotion, and what I see is a combination of disappointment and resignation. I should have expected it, in fact, I think I did expect it, but I can't help feeling hurt by his response. I wanted him to share my enthusiasm for this last phase of remodeling, the first phase that I've truly been excited about, but I know that I haven't earned his trust. He expects we'll have to shell out more money to hire professionals to complete the project once I lose my enthusiasm for it.

To be fair to him, I've refused to trust that some of the changes he's made in himself for the sake of our marriage—like becoming less of a perfectionist and a micromanager—are permanent. But I'm beginning to understand how frustrating that must be for him, that over time we all change. And you need to let your spouse change. I can't keep holding on to who he was in the past.

"You're not going to finish this," Matt says. His words, I know, are carefully chosen. He's probably calculating how much we will have to spend to have professionals finish this job for us.

"You have to let me change," I say quietly. "You have to give me a chance to show you that I'm different." He doesn't respond at first.

"You need to trust me," I say, my voice stronger this time, and he looks at the walls, at my face, at his hands.

"I will trust you," he says, and walks out. We don't talk about the kitchen for the rest of the night. Rather, he tells me about his day, while I share stories about mine.

The next morning, I make a project list. At Home Depot I purchase all of my supplies—paint, brushes, masks, and sandpaper—and rent a steamer. At home, with a screwdriver I remove all of the fixtures, which I seal up in a plastic bag. Then I work all day, my fingernails breaking and bleeding as I try to scrub the glue from around the windowsill. An hour before Matt is due home, I bag up all of the wallpaper that has dropped to the floor, using the shop vac to get the smaller pieces, and wipe the glue from the tile.

When Matt returns home, he heads straight for the kitchen. He pretends that he needs a glass of water, but I know he's really checking on my progress. But I don't care. I've finished two of the walls, and I know he'll be relieved and impressed by my progress. "It looks great in here," he says, tapping his fingers against the Sheetrock. By the third day, he no longer goes directly into the kitchen.

At last, I've prepped the walls and am ready to begin painting. I make a few strokes on the far wall. The color I've selected, terra-cotta, doesn't have the rose undertones that I thought it would. It's orange, bright orange, like a plastic Halloween pumpkin. When we painted our master bath, I changed my mind so many times as to what color I wanted that we ended up with eight pints of different shades of paint. I refuse to make that mistake again. So our kitchen will be orange.

Five days later, with no fingernails left, I finish painting the kitchen. Surprisingly enough, the color works well with our pale yellow cabinetry and trim. It gives the kitchen a warmth it lacked before. For the final touches, I buy shadow boxes, a painting, and a chalkboard at Target.

Matt loves it. We've stopped eating in the dining room and have breakfast, sometimes dinner even, in the kitchen instead. "I am really impressed with you," he says whenever he looks at the walls. And I feel good about myself, too. Change is possible; you need to recognize it in your spouse, rather than continuously punishing them for past mistakes.

The next weekend, we invite friends over for dinner, eager to show off our remodeled kitchen.

"I love the color in here!" one woman exclaims. "It's so bold and daring. However did you come up with it?"

Matt smiles and shrugs. "My wife," he says proudly. "She's an artist."

FIFTY-ONE

Work in Progress

It is a lovely thing to have a husband and wife
developing together. That is what marriage really
means; helping one another to reach the full status
of being persons, responsible and autonomous
beings who do not run away from life.
—Paul Tournier

Nine hundred and fifty dollars?" Matt asks, setting our two-page credit card bill on the dining room table in front of me. How could I, the cheapskate, have spent that much money? He's circled all of my discretionary spending in red, the hundreds of dollars I've allegedly spent at Target, Linens 'n Things, and Pier 1. For a moment, I think there must be some sort of error, that our credit card was stolen, perhaps.

"How is that possible?" I ask, looking around our home, desperate to point out the objects that I've purchased so that he doesn't think I've simply squandered our hard-earned money: beaded lamps, a mirror, five candles, two candleholders, bedroom shelves, a candelabrum for the living room, serving utensils, slipcovers, table linens, and, my biggest purchase of all, a black slate console table for the entryway. I've bought so many items over the past few weeks that Matt, upon returning home from work, proudly proclaimed I had turned into Mrs. Suzy Homemaker. Reduced to a stereotype, I argued with him, but, later that night, I wondered, was that what I had become? And, if so, was it that bad?

And now, Matt pats my shoulder reassuringly. "Dear, I don't want to discourage you. You know that I think you've done a wonderful job with our home," he says. Using red and green throw pillows and blankets, I've tied together our miasma of traditional, contemporary, and modern furniture that we've collected through family and friends. "But please be aware of how much you are spending."

I appreciate his kindness in his choice of words. In the past, he would have reacted to the bill, and I would have reacted to him. But we've realized that you waste your energy getting worked up over every issue. We've stopped taking our disputes and our differences so personally. Our disagreements escalate much slower now, if at all. And once our point is made, we let go of it.

"I think I'm done spending for a while," I say to Matt. I think that bill is harder on me than it is on him. "Do you want me to return some of what I bought?"

He hesitates and looks around us. "No, leave it," he says. I know how pleased he is that I've finally taken an interest in our home. And I'm proud that over the past year, I've helped create not only a comfortable home for us but a marriage that is as solid as its walls.

What I've discovered is that remodeling your home is much like building your marriage. You won't necessarily have the skills you need going in, but you'll learn quickly enough. In the same way that I experienced much confusion and uncertainty adjusting to my role as a new wife, so did I feel overwhelmed trying to figure out what would and wouldn't work for us in our new home. If we ripped up our old carpet, what would we replace it with? If we tore down all of the mirrors, what would we hang on the bare walls? My uncertainty paralyzed me from making any decisions. I knew which colors and style of furniture I didn't like, but I couldn't choose from what remained, and so I rarely made a purchase while in a store. But then, with Matt's encouragement, I began to experiment with paints and fabrics and discovered that I liked rich, solid colors—no pastels or patterns.

While remodeling, we made plenty of mistakes. The carpet we put in the master bedroom shows every speck of dirt that lands on it, and, even when we vacuum, there is only a short period of time before it looks dirty again. A bookcase I thought would fit nicely in our living room we quickly retired to our office. And the same is true of our marriage, where we often erred while trying to relate to one another. But, after awhile, as we became more adept, both home remodeling and our marriage simultaneously grew easier and more rewarding for me. I learned that just as in your marriage, you need to be willing to take risks when home remodeling. And, here I am now, having spent more money on one shopping spree than I have over our entire first year.

Most of all, what I've learned is that both our house and our marriage are works in progress. Your home is constantly evolving to fit a new trend, a new piece of furniture, a new color. And sometimes you just don't have the patience to tackle that last room and so you put it off, or perhaps you realize what you did didn't work and must be redone. In a parallel fashion, your marriage is constantly evolving to carefully balance your needs, which change over time, with your spouse's. What works for you and your spouse now may not down the road. But what I've learned is that it doesn't matter whether your home or your marriage looks like anybody else's. What matters is that it suits the two of you, that it's yours. And for all of the improvements and adjustments we've made over the past year, I must say that we're better people for it.

FIFTY-TWO

Marriage Is a Leap of Faith

Love is not a matter of counting the years; it is making the years count.

—William Smith

Happy anniversary," I say to myself, as I sit alone on our leather sofa picking chocolate chip cookie dough chunks from my Ben & Jerry's ice cream. Matt is in Boca Raton, Florida, for a two-week trial, where he says the sweltering heat makes his suit feel like a fur coat. But he has sent me a dozen fragrant red roses that have gloriously opened up. They look fresh and beautiful displayed on our dining room table.

Feeling guilty for eating a pint of ice cream, I decide to go for a run before darkness settles. Before Matt and I met, I was a marathon runner. Now, as I jog around our neighborhood, I think about how much the first year of marriage is like running your first marathon. Often, you're unprepared for both, but you learn as you go.

What I discovered in marathon running that applies to my marriage as well is that your choice of a spouse makes all the difference. You need to find somebody who is about your pace, who can support you, otherwise you may grow bored having to constantly slow down for him or you may feel inept struggling to keep up. As a first-time marathoner, you often finish only as a team. If one of you falls off pace, you both do—and that run is much harder alone. Halfway up a hill you may need your running partner's encouragement, and halfway down the hill he or she may need yours. If you try to beat your partner to the finish line, you may ruin your pace or theirs. And over time you learn to let go of your layers of self-protection—it's easier to run with a lighter load. Just as in marriage, trust your partner to support your needs. Together you will strive to reach that finish line, encountering all sorts of obstacles, frustrations, and disappointments, all the while hoping you don't pass out before you reach it. But that, too, is part of the thrill of marriage. It is your spouse who helps keep your universe in balance for you, who holds your hand, wipes your tears, and simply laughs with you. And so it is not, "And two become one." It's, "And two become a team."

In marriage, you can't always know what sort of obstacles you will encounter over the years that are out of your control—the death of your parents, an ill family member, a financial hardship, or a midlife crisis—just as in marathon running, where you cannot control what race day will bring—a stomachache, a storm, a blister. On some stretches you may find yourself running blindly, with sweat in your eyes, but if you just stay on track, if you just show up every day and do your best, eventually your strain will give way to what's known as runner's high.

And that is why it's important to work hard during your first year of marriage. In the same way that you train so that you know at which pace you should run so that you do not burn out too early but you still cross the finish line with a respectable time, which clothes to wear so that your skin doesn't chafe or blister, and how to build up enough endurance so that you can make it all twenty-six miles, so, too, should you train hard during your first year of marriage so that you know how to tackle your problems and differences before life's real burdens hit. You'll set the patterns and behaviors for the years to come. Sometimes your partner will push you, challenging you with his opposing point of view, but you'll soon adapt to your new pace. You've developed stamina and are a stronger person for it. And while it may be difficult to see the results of working hard in the short term, remember that what you do during your training period will determine whether your final test of endurance is easy or difficult, contentious or amicable. Foundations are established in the beginning. Don't bog down your marriage with bad energy before it even gets a chance to get started.

I finished my first marathon with a respectable time. I felt powerful, unstoppable, and free, having reached my goal. I knew that with better training, had I sped up instead of slowed down when my muscles ached or forced myself to train on days I felt too tired to drive to the gym, I could have done a little better, run a little faster, perhaps qualified for the Boston Marathon even. And that is how I feel on our one-year anniversary. I wish I had worked harder during our first year of marriage, as today it is an invaluable source of strength for me. Matt makes any pressure I feel from the outside world bearable. There is no place that I feel safer than in our marriage. I was overcome with love just hearing his voice when he called in to wish me a happy anniversary.

Anne has a theory that at the one-year mark all of your problems magically disappear, like your penance is over and you can start enjoying your marriage now. But I think that her theory is a credit to her. She and her husband, Pete, have set a firm foundation for resolving their differences. They each spend less time worrying about what the other is contributing to their marriage and more time just helping each other through the day.

None of us—not Anne, Brenda, Christina, or me—have the perfect love story. Nor do we have the perfect husbands or the perfect lives or the perfect selves. But what we've learned is that you don't need the perfect love or the perfect person when you walk down the aisle. What you need is the right material with which to work.

We all struggled through our first year of marriage. We were all surprised by the time and effort that our marriages took. But by accepting the challenges in our marriages—the disappointments, the loneliness, the frustrations—we have all grown into stronger, better people. And today we spend less time keeping score, marking our individual victories, and more time loving each other. We've developed flexible marriages in which we can comfortably work out problems and situations that may arise. What we've all learned is that perfection does not exist. Fulfillment does.

And that is my confession: I like myself better in marriage. I feel truly happy and completed by Matt, and I don't want to think about making it through life alone. Matt has indissolubly become a part of me. The better part, maybe.

Bibliography

I relied heavily on the following texts:

Bloom, Linda, and Charlie Bloom. *101 Things I Wish I Knew When I Got Married: Simple Lessons to Make Love Last.* New World Library, 2004.

Carlson, Richard. *A Don't Sweat the Small Stuff Treasury: A Special Collection for Newlyweds.* Hyperion, 2000.

Neuman, M. Gary. *Emotional Infidelity: How to Avoid It and 10 Other Secrets to a Great Marriage.* Crown, 2001.

Niven, David, Ph.D. *The 100 Simple Secrets of Great Relationships: What Scientists Have Learned and How You Can Use It.* HarperSanFrancisco, 2003.

Paul, Pamela. *The Starter Marriage and the Future of Matrimony.* Random House, 2003.

Roiphe, Anne. *Married: A Fine Predicament.* Basic Books, 2002.

Jennifer Jeanne Patterson received her M.F.A. in creative writing from Columbia University. She is the author of a syndicated column called *Newlyweds,* which has appeared in *Minnesota Bride* and *The Ithaca Journal* and on Lovetripper.com.